U.S. Department of State

Security Guidelines for Traveling & Living Overseas

This book is a compilation of security guidelines, developed by the U.S. Department of State, for U.S. Citizens traveling and living overseas.

Effective security precautions require a continuous and conscious awareness of your environment. This is especially true when living in a foreign country where it will be necessary to adapt to new cultures, customs, and laws which, in most instances, are very different from those to which America.

The implementation of security guidelines contained in this publication could reduce the vulnerability of American private sector personnel and enterprises abroad to criminal or terrorist acts.

- Personal Security Guidelines for the American Business Traveler Overseas

- The Overseas Security Advisory Council's Travel Safety Reference Guide

- 11 Best Practices for Crisis Preparedness

- Security Guidelines for American Families Living Abroad

- Security Guidelines for American Enterprises Abroad

Personal Security Guidelines for the American Business Traveler Overseas

Introduction

Effective security precautions require a continuous and conscious awareness of your environment. This is especially true when visiting a foreign country where it will be necessary to adapt to new cultures, customs, and laws, which, in many instances, are very different from those to which Americans are accustomed in the United States.

The implementation of security guidelines contained in this publication should reduce the vulnerability of American private sector personnel traveling abroad to criminal or terrorist acts. Individuals should ensure, however, that any approach chosen is best suited for their individual situation.

Chapter I. Introduction

This booklet was developed to inform and make the American business traveler aware of the potentially hostile overseas environment in which they may be traveling or working. The information contained in this booklet will familiarize the traveler with personal security guidelines for traveling overseas. The potential hazards and vulnerabilities that are inherent in protecting/carrying sensitive or proprietary information while traveling are described, as are surveillance and/or targeting recognition, personal conduct abroad, hostage/hijacking survival and fire safety.

There are several scenarios to traveling abroad that are addressed: first, the actual getting from point A to B; second, the airport; third, the hotel or temporary quarters; fourth, traveling within a foreign country; and, lastly, the office or workplace. Each of these five situations presents different potential security problems.

The most effective means of protecting yourself and your property is the liberal use of common sense reinforced with a high state of security awareness. Do not give anyone the opportunity to exploit vulnerabilities. Stay alert and exercise good judgment.

Chapter II. Travel Preparation and Planning

Travel Itinerary

DO NOT publicize your travel plans, but limit that knowledge to those who need to know. Leave a full itinerary of your travel schedule, hotel phone numbers and business appointments with your office and with a family member or friend.

Passport

Is it valid? Are the visas current for the country of destination? If not, you and everything in your possession may be looked at in-depth by host government authorities. If you are carrying documents that are sensitive or proprietary, they will be examined in detail to see if there is anything that would be of interest. If there is, you can bet that copies will be made, and there is not much that you will be able to do about it.

Make photocopies of your passport, visa and other important documents that you will be traveling with. Put copies in both your carry on and checked luggage. This makes it easier to replace your identification documents should anything happen. (Also, it is a good idea to leave a photocopy with someone at home.)

Visas

Is a visa required for any of the countries that you are visiting and do you have the appropriate visa(s)? Is the information on your visa application true and correct? In some countries, falsifying information on a visa application can result in an unexpected vacation in the local bastilles.

Some countries are sensitive to which visa you obtain. If you are traveling on business, a business visa should be obtained; otherwise a tourist visa is acceptable.

Medical

Take plenty of any prescription medication with you, as well as an extra set of eyeglasses or contact lenses. Also, take a copy of your prescription should you need to have glasses, contacts or medication replaced. Keep an inoculation record and update it before each trip as each country has different requirements.

- Carry with you a list with your blood type, allergies, medical conditions and special requirements. It is a good idea to have a medical alert bracelet if you have a special medical condition.

- Inoculations - Does the country to be visited require any specific inoculations? This information is available from the embassy or consulate. Be sure to carry your international shot record, just in case.

- If you do not have comprehensive medical coverage, consider enrolling in an international health program. Hospitals in foreign countries do not take credit cards and most will not honor U.S. based medical insurance plans.

Miscellaneous

Keep your personal affairs up to date. If possible, leave a power of attorney with a family member or friend should anything happen to you.

- Do research on the country you will be traveling to before you go. Talk with friends, family or business associates who have visited the country. They can usually give you some good tips for your trip. Also, for any travel warnings or other conditions that you should be aware of, check with the U.S. State Department, Bureau of Consular Affairs.

- Travelers should discuss with their travel agents, which airlines, hotels and car rental companies are recommended.

- Carry in your wallet/pocketbook only the documents you will need. Take only the credit cards you plan to use on your trip.

- If you plan to rent a car, check to see if you must obtain an international drivers permit for the country you plan to visit.

- Obtain information from U.S. Customs regarding any special requirements for the country you are visiting.

Local Import Restrictions

Request from the embassy of the country you plan to visit a copy of any list or pamphlet describing customs restrictions or banned materials. This is a hint designed to minimize the possibility of an encounter with the local authorities.

Leave all expensive and heirloom jewelry at home.

Luggage

DO NOT pack sensitive or proprietary information in your checked luggage. Double envelope the material and hand carry it. Be sure that your luggage is tagged with covered tags that protect your address from open observation. Put your name and address inside each piece of luggage and be sure that all luggage is locked or secured in some fashion.

Luggage Locks

The locks on your luggage are not that secure when it comes to the professional thief or manipulator and are really no more than a deterrent. But, if time is of the essence to the perpetrator, and it usually is when a crime is involved, there are a couple of suggestions that might deter surreptitious entry and/or theft.

- For added security on all luggage, run a strip of nylon filament tape around the suitcase to preclude its opening accidentally if dropped or mistreated by baggage handlers.

- For luggage and briefcases with two combination locks, reset the combination locks from the factory combination (000) to different combinations on each of the right and left locks.

- For luggage with single locks, set the lock on each piece of luggage with a different combination.

- DO NOT pack extra glasses or necessary daily medication in your luggage. Carry it in your briefcase, purse or pocket. If you are the victim of a hijacking, you may need these items - if they are in your luggage, you probably will not be able to get to them.

- On your luggage use your business address and telephone number. If possible, use a closed name tag with a cover. Do not use a laminated business card on your luggage, and avoid putting the company name or any logos on your luggage.

- Check with the airline and/or your personal insurance company regarding any lost luggage coverage.

- Make sure you use sturdy luggage. Do not over pack as the luggage could open if dropped. Bind the luggage with strapping so that it will remain intact.

- Never place your valuables (jewelry, money and travelers checks) in your checked luggage. Never leave your bags unattended.

- Consider obtaining a modest amount of foreign currency before you leave your home country. Criminals often watch for and target international travelers purchasing large amounts of foreign currency at airport banks and currency exchange windows.

Airline Security and Seat Selection

- Try to book a non-stop flight, as these have fewer takeoffs and landings.

- Choose an airline with a good safety and on-time record.

- Try to make your stopovers in airports that have a high security standard and good security screening.

- Try to fly wide body planes. Hijackers tend to avoid these as having too many passengers.

- Most travelers prefer an aisle seat. Choose a window or center seat. This will keep you away from the hijackers and any action that may be happening in the aisle.

Chapter III. At The Airport

To diminish the risks of becoming an innocent bystander victim of a terrorist attack and reduce your exposure to the criminal threat, there are a number of things that you should remember when checking into an airport.

- In the event of a disturbance of any kind, go in the opposite direction. DO NOT GET INVOLVED!

- Plan to check in early for your flight to avoid long lines at the ticket counter.

- Go directly to the gate or secure area after checking your luggage. (Secure Zone - Area between security/immigration and the departure gate.) Avoid waiting rooms and shopping areas outside the secure areas.

- Stay away from glass wall areas and airport coffee shops which are open to the concourse or public waiting areas.

- From the time you pack your luggage until you check it with the carrier at the airport maintain positive control of all items, both hand carried and checked.

- At many airports security personnel, following FAA protocol, will ask you questions about control of your luggage. Know what items you are carrying and be able to describe any/all electrical items.

- When going through the pre-board screening process cooperate with security personnel and remember that they are there to help ensure that your travel is safe.

- When arriving at or departing from an airport it is a good idea not to be exchanging items between bags while waiting in line for security screening or immigration/customs processing. Complete all packing before entering such areas.

- If a conflict should arise while undergoing the screening process, cooperate. Obtain the names of the screeners involved, and then discuss the matter with a supervisor from the appropriate air carrier.

- Remember that x-ray will not damage film, videos or computer equipment. Many times such items can be cleared using x-ray which means that they will not have to be handled by the screener.

- Consider being transported to/from the airport by a hotel vehicle. Generally, the cost is not prohibitive, and arrangements can be made in advance by your travel agent.

- Declare all currency and negotiable instruments as required by law.

- NEVER leave your luggage or briefcase unattended, even while checking in or once in the secure zone. In some countries, the police or security forces assume that an unattended bag is a bomb, and your luggage could be forcefully opened or even destroyed.

- Always be aware of where you are in conjunction with where you are going. If an incident occurs, you need to know how to avoid it and either get out of the area or to your boarding area.

- Dress casually when traveling, as this will keep any undue attention from you. Once aboard the flight, remove your shoes for better circulation. Walk around the flight cabin to keep your blood circulating and swelling down.

- Avoid last minute dashes to the airport.

- Eat moderately, avoid alcoholic beverages and drink plenty of water as this will help to avoid dehydration.

- If possible, before you leave make an effort to adjust your sleep patterns.

- Sleep as much as possible during the flight.

- Carry airsickness medication with you. Even the best traveler sometimes experiences airsickness.

- Avoid a demanding schedule upon arrival. Give yourself a chance to adjust to your surroundings.

Chapter IV. Selecting a Secure Hotel

Many U.S. corporations have hotels abroad that are owned by local businessmen and staffed by local workers but managed by first class U.S. hoteliers. You usually can expect levels of safety and security that are consistent with U.S. standards.

- Ask the corporate travel agent for a list of recommended hotels.

- Check with the Regional Security Officer at the U.S. Embassy for a list of hotels utilized by officials visiting the area.

Making Reservations

Make your own reservations when practical and consistent with company policies. The fewer people that become involved in your travel and lodging arrangements, the better.

- If traveling abroad, especially in politically sensitive areas, consider making reservations using your employer's street address, without identifying the company, and using your personal credit card. Again, the less known about your travel itinerary, and whom you represent, the better.

- If arriving after 6:00 P.M., ensure that reservations are guaranteed.

- Request information about parking arrangements if anticipating renting an automobile.

- Be aware that credit card information has been compromised in the past. Always audit monthly credit card statements to ensure that unauthorized use has not been made of your account.

- It is advisable to join frequent travelers' programs available with many lodging companies. These programs enable upgrades to executive or concierge floors where available. Be sure to advise the person taking reservations that you are a member and request an upgrade.

Arriving at or Departing From the Hotel

The most vulnerable part of your journey is traveling between the point of debarkation/embarkation and the hotel. Do not linger or wander unnecessarily in the parking lot, indoor garage or public space around the hotel - be alert for suspicious persons and behavior. Watch for distractions that are intentionally staged to setup a pickpocket, luggage theft or purse snatch.

- Stay with your luggage until it is brought into the lobby, or placed into the taxi or limo.

- Consider using the bellman. Luggage in the "care, custody and control" of the hotel causes the hotel to be liable for your property. Protect claim checks; they are your evidence!

- Keep in mind though that there are limits of liability created by states and countries to protect hoteliers. Personal travel documents, lap tops, jewelry, and other valuables and sensitive documents in excess of $1,000 in value should be hand carried and personally protected.

- If you arrive by auto, park as close to a hotel access point as possible, and park in a lighted area. Remove all property from the car interior and place it in the trunk. Avoid leaving valuables or personal documents in the glove compartment. Prior to leaving the security of the vehicle, note any suspicious persons or behavior.

- If using valet service, leave only the ignition key, and take trunk, house, or office keys with you. Often, valets are not employees of the hotel and work for contract firms.

- Parking garages are difficult to secure. Avoid dimly lit garages that are not patrolled and do not have security telephones or intercoms.

- Female travelers should consider asking for an escort to their vehicles whether parked in the lot or garage.

Registration

In some countries, your passport may be temporarily held by the hotel for review by the police or other authorities, obtain its return at the earliest possible time.

- Be aware of persons in the hotel lobby who may have unusual interest in your arrival.

- If carrying your luggage, keep it within view or touch. One recommendation is to position luggage against your leg during registration but place a briefcase or a purse on the desk or counter in front of you.

- Ground floor rooms, which open to a pool area or beach with sliding glass doors and window access, are considered vulnerable. Depending upon the situation, area, and security coverage, exercise a higher level of security if assigned a first-floor room.

- It is suggested that female travelers request rooms that are away from the elevator landing and stairwells. This is to avoid being caught by surprise by persons exiting the elevator with you or hiding in the stairwell.

- Always accept bellman assistance upon check-in. Allow the bellman to open the room, turn lights on, and check the room to ensure that it is vacant and ready for your stay. Before dismissing the bellman, always inspect the door lock, locks on sliding glass doors, optical viewer, privacy latch or chain, guest room safes, dead bolt lock on interconnecting suite door, and telephone. If a discrepancy is found, request a room change.

- Ask where the nearest fire stairwell is located. Make a mental note which direction you must turn and approximately how many steps there are to the closest fire stairwell. In the event of a fire, there is frequently dense smoke and no lighting.

- Also observe where the nearest house telephone is located in case of an emergency. Determine if the telephone is configured in such a manner that anyone can dial a guest room directly, or whether the phone is connected to the switchboard. Most security-conscious hotels require a caller to identify whom they are attempting to telephone rather than providing a room number.

- Note how hotel staff are uniformed and identified. Many "pretext" crimes occur by persons misrepresenting themselves as hotel employees on house telephones to gain access to guest rooms. Avoid permitting a person into the guest room unless you have confirmed that the person is authorized to enter. This can be verified by using the optical viewer and by calling the front desk.

Chapter V. In Your Hotel

All hotel rooms abroad are bugged for audio and visual surveillance. This statement, of course, is NOT TRUE, but that is the premise under which you must operate to maintain an adequate level of security awareness while conducting business abroad. Many hotel rooms overseas are under surveillance. In those countries where the intelligence services are very active, if you are a business person working for an American company of interest to the government or government sponsored competitor, everything that you do in that hotel room may be recorded and analyzed for possible vulnerabilities or for any useful information that can be derived from your conversation.

With the basic premise established above, here are some security tips that will minimize the potential risks.

Hotel Room Key

Keep it with you at all times. The two most common ways that thieves and others use to determine if a person is in their hotel room is to look at the hotel room mail slot or key board or call the room on the house phone. If you do not answer the phone that is one thing, but, if your room key is there, you are obviously out and the coast is clear for a thief or anyone else who is interested in searching your room and luggage.

Upon Arrival

Invest in a good map of the city. Mark significant points on a map such as your hotel, embassies and police stations. Study the map and make a mental note of alternative routes to your hotel or local office should your map become lost or stolen.

- Be aware of your surroundings. Look up and down the street before exiting a building.

- Learn how to place a telephone call and how to use the coin telephones. Make sure you always have extra coins for the telephone.

- Avoid jogging or walking in cities you are not familiar with. If you must jog, be aware of the traffic patterns when crossing public streets. (Joggers have been seriously injured by failing to understand local traffic conditions.)

Valuables

Valuables should normally be left at home. The rule of thumb is, if you neither want nor can afford to lose them, DO NOT TAKE THEM! However, if you must carry valuables, the best way to protect them is to secure them in your local offices. If that is not possible, the next best course of action is to seal any valuables by double enveloping, initialing across seams and taping all edges and seams before depositing them in the hotel's safe deposit box or safe.

Luggage

Keep it locked whenever you are out of the room. It will not stop the professional thief or intelligence agent but it will keep the curious maid honest.

Passport

Keep your passport with you at all times. The only time that you should relinquish it is:

- To the hotel if required by law when registering.

- If you are required to identify yourself to local authorities for any reason.

At night, lock your passport and your other valuables in your luggage. This eliminates their mysterious disappearance while you are asleep or in the shower.

Utilize a portable or improvised burglar alarm while asleep. Two ash trays and a water glass are quite effective as an alarm when placed on the floor in front of the entry door into your room. Place a water glass in one ashtray and put the second ashtray on top of the glass. If a straight chair is available, place it next to the door and put the ash tray/water glass alarm on the edge of the chair where it will fall with enough racket to wake you.

Chapter VI. Guest Room as a "Safe Haven"

Hotels are required to provide reasonable care to ensure that guests have a safe and secure stay. Hotels are not required to guarantee guest security. You are responsible for your personal security and property.

- While in the room, keep the door closed and engage the dead bolt and privacy latch or chain. A limited number of hotel emergency keys can override the dead bolt locks. To ensure privacy use the latch or chain!

- Hoteliers provide guest room "safes" for the convenience of guests. However, these containers are not as durable as bank safes and can be breached. Furthermore, the Housekeepers Liability Laws provide that if guest property is not in the "care, custody and control of the hotel," the hotel is not liable. Guests should always place money or valuables in the safe deposit box at the front desk of the hotel.

- When leaving the guest room, ensure that the door properly closes and is secured. Make a mental note of how your property was left; avoid leaving valuables in plain view or in an unorganized manner. A number of hotel employees enter the room each day to clean, repair and restock the room. Although most hotel employees are honest and hardworking, a few succumb to the temptation of cash or jewelry left unprotected.

- If you determine that an item is missing, conduct a thorough search prior to reporting the incident to hotel security. Do not expect to receive a copy of the security report, as it is an internal document. The incident should be reported to the local police, the Regional Security and Consular Officers at the U.S. Embassy, and your insurance carrier. Hotel security can provide a letter verifying that you reported property missing.

- Prior to traveling, it is recommended that you copy all credit cards, passport, air tickets and other documents to facilitate reporting loss and replacing them. While traveling abroad, secure these documents in the room safe deposit box and carry copies of your passport and visa.

- Request housekeeping make up your room while you are at breakfast, rather than leave a "Please Service This Room" sign on the door knob. This sign is a signal to criminals that the room is unoccupied.

- If you are required to use parking stickers in your auto, be sure that it does not indicate your name or room number.

Chapter VII. Around The Hotel

Most first-class international hotels have spent a considerable sum to ensure your safety and security. Fire safety equipment, CCTVs, and security patrols are often part of the hotel's security plan. Regardless of the level of security provided by the hotel, you need to become familiar with certain aspects of the security profile of the hotel. This will take on increased significance when you may be forced to stay at the only hotel at a particular location.

- Vary the time and route by which you leave and return to the hotel. Be alert for persons watching your movements.

- Note if hotel security locks certain access points after dark. Plan to use the main entrance upon return to the property.

- Speak with the bellman, concierge and front desk regarding safe areas around the city in which to jog, dine or sightsee. Ask about local customs and which taxi companies to use or avoid.

- Do not take valuables to the spa or work out room. Note if there are house phones available in the event of a confrontation or emergency.

- Be cautious when entering rest rooms in the hotel. On occasion, unauthorized persons use these facilities to deal drugs or engage in prostitution or theft. Female travelers should be alert to placing purses on hangers on the inside of the lavatory doors, or on the floor in stalls - two frequent locations for grab and run thefts.

- Criminals often use areas around public telephones to stage pickpocket activity or theft. Keep briefcases and purses in view or "in touch" while using phones. Caution is urged in safeguarding telephone credit card numbers. Criminals wait for callers to announce credit card numbers on public phones and then sell the numbers for unauthorized use.

- Purse snatchers and briefcase thieves are known to work hotel bars and restaurants waiting for unknowing guests to drape these items on chairs or under tables only to discover them missing as they are departing. Keep items in view or "in touch". Be alert to scams involving an unknown person spilling a drink or food on your clothing. An accomplice may be preparing to steal your wallet, briefcase or purse.

- The pool or beach area is a fertile area for thieves to take advantage of guests enjoying recreation. Leave valuables in the hotel. Safeguard your room key and camera. Sign for food and beverages on your room bill rather than carry cash.

- Prostitutes take advantage of travelers around the world through various ploys, use of "knock out" drugs, and theft from the victim's room. Avoid engaging persons who you do not know and refrain from inviting them to your guest room.

Chapter VIII. Fire Safety for the Traveler

Fire safety at home and abroad is a matter of thinking ahead, knowing what to do, and keeping your fear under control. Panic and smoke are the most dangerous threats in the case of a fire. To minimize the risk of a fire, the traveler should remember the precautions listed below and where feasible:

- Stay only at hotels, which have smoke detectors and/or sprinklers installed in all rooms and provide information about fire/safety procedures.

- Request a room between the second and seventh floor. Most fire departments do not have the capability to rescue people above the seventh-floor level with external rescue equipment (i.e., ladders).

- Inquire as to how guests are notified if there is an emergency.

Your Hotel Room

- Note the location of the fire exits (stairs) on your floor. Count the number of doors between your room and the exit. If there is a fire, you may have to crawl there in the dark.

- Check exit doors to be sure that they are unlocked and that stairwells are clear of obstructions.

- Note the location of fire alarms, extinguishers and hoses and read any fire safety information available in your room.

- Check outside your room window to ascertain if there is a possible escape route that would be feasible in an extreme emergency.

In Case of a Fire

- KEEP CALM - DO NOT PANIC.

- Call the front desk and notify them of the location of the fire.

- Check your door by placing your palm on the door and then on the doorknob. If either feels hot, DO NOT OPEN THE DOOR.

- If it is safe to exit from your room, head for the stairs. TAKE YOUR ROOM KEY WITH YOU; YOU MAY HAVE TO RETURN TO YOUR ROOM.

- If the corridor is full of smoke, crawl to the exit and again check the door before opening it to see if it is hot. The fire could be in the stairwell.

- DO NOT USE THE ELEVATOR!

- If you cannot leave your room or the stairwells are unsafe and you must return to your room:

- Notify the front desk that you are in your room awaiting rescue.

- Open a window for fresh air. Do not break the window as you may need to close it again if smoke starts to enter from the outside.

- Fill the tub and sink with water. Soak towels and blankets as necessary to block vents and openings around doors to keep the smoke and fumes out.

- Attempt to keep the walls, doors and towels covering vents and cracks cool and wet.

- A wet towel swung around the room will help clear the room of smoke.

- Cover your mouth and nose with a wet cloth.

- Stay low, but alert to any signs of rescue from the street or the halls. Let the firemen know where you are by waving a towel or sheet out the window.

Chapter IX. In The Work Place

The work place, your home away from home. Here you are safe and secure in the one place where you no longer have to worry about what you do or say. WRONG! You can be just as vulnerable here as anywhere else in the country. You probably are safer, but there are still some precautions that should be taken.

- Safeguard all sensitive or proprietary papers and documents; do not leave them lying around in the office or on top of a desk.

- Guard your conversations so that unauthorized personnel are not able to eavesdrop on discussions pertaining to proprietary information, personnel issues or management planning or problems. In many countries, employees are debriefed by the local intelligence or security services in an effort to learn as much as possible about activities of American companies and their personnel.

- Be careful of all communications. Be aware that the monitoring of telephone, telegraph and international mail is not uncommon in some countries.

Chapter X. Traveling By Train

In many countries, railroads continue to offer a safe, reliable and comfortable means of travel between major metropolitan areas. Other countries, however, operate rail systems that use antiquated equipment, are often overcrowded and seldom run on time. As a general rule, the more advanced (socially and economically) a country is, the more modern and reliable will be its rail service. Frequently, rail travel provides a more economical method of travel than other modes of transportation, and frequently it is the only available transportation to smaller cities and towns. However, rail travel can present some security risks to the traveler, just like other means of travel.

Railroads are "soft" targets for several types of criminal or terrorist attacks. They operate over open ground and are easily accessible to the public. The tracks on which the trains operate are in the open for most of the distance they cover. This easy accessibility provides an inviting target for bombings and other forms of sabotage.

The railroad terminals and stations are like self-contained cities, open to the public, frequently for 24 hours a day. They provide a fertile ground for pickpockets, purse snatchers, baggage thieves, bombers and other criminals to operate.

Likewise, trains themselves offer similar opportunities to criminals and terrorists. A train is like a hotel on wheels, offering temporary accommodations, such as restaurants, sleeping space, bars and lounges. All of these can be, and often times are, subject to criminal activities including robbery, thievery, bombing and even, albeit rarely, hostage taking.

Security Risks

Generally, railroad terminals and trains are easy targets for the following types of attacks:

- Bombing and other forms of sabotage to railroad tracks, terminals and trains;

- Robberies and burglaries;

- Theft of unattended baggage on board trains and in rail terminals; and

- Thefts from sleeping compartments.

- Just as air travel calls for planning and preparation to lessen the risks of unfortunate experiences while traveling, rail travel also requires certain preventive measures in order to lessen the likelihood of the traveler becoming a victim. Some of these simple, yet effective, precautions can help make a rail trip a comfortable and convenient means of moving between or within many countries of the world.

Some Precautionary Measures

Prior to Departure:

- It should be noted that many cities have more than one railroad station. Travelers should confirm in advance from which station your train will depart. Make certain that you use the right one.

- Make reservations in advance so that you do not have to stand in the frequently long lines at the rail station ticket counters. This is where pickpockets, baggage thieves and purse-snatchers like to operate. Your hotel concierge can assist in making your reservations and picking up your ticket.

- Travel light and always keep your luggage under your control. In the time it takes to set down your luggage to check a timetable, a baggage thief can make off with it.

- Watch your tickets. Keep them in an inside pocket or purse to lessen the chance that they can be stolen.

- Do not discard your train ticket until completion of your trip and you have left the arrival area. In some countries you will be required to show your ticket at the exit of the arrival station. If you do not have it, you may be required to purchase another one. Hold on to your ticket, whether or not a conductor checks it.

- Make certain that you board the right car and that it is going to your intended destination.

- Find out in advance if your car will have to be switched to another train en route, when and where this will occur, and the name of the stop just prior to the switching point; be prepared accordingly.

- If you have to transfer to another train to reach your destination, determine this in advance and know where you will make the transfer, the time of transfer, and the train number and departure time of your connecting train (and the track number if possible).

- Learn how to tell if you are in the correct car and if it goes to your destination. Name boards on the side of the car will tell you this.

For example, a name board that appears like this:

VENEZIA

Bologna - Firenze

ROMA

shows that the car began in Venice, stops in Bologna and Florence, and terminates in Rome. Next to the steps leading into the car you should see the numeral "1" or "2", or both. The "1" indicates First Class; the "2" indicates Second Class; and "1" at one end of the car and "2" at the other indicates one part of the car is First Class and the other is Second Class.

- Make certain you know how to spell and pronounce the name of your destination city so you can recognize it when announced.

- Be alert to train splitting. This occurs when part of the train is split off and attached to another train while the remainder of the original train then continues on its way. Check with the ticket agent or on-board conductor to determine this.

- Try not to schedule a late night or early morning arrival. You might find yourself stranded at a rail station with no public transportation.

- Arrange to be met at your arrival point whenever possible.

On Board the Train

- If possible, check unneeded luggage into the baggage car.

- Keep your luggage with you at all times. If you must leave your seat, either take the luggage with you or secure it to your seat or the baggage rack with a strong cable-lock.

- Try to get a window seat. This provides a quick means of escape in the event of an accident.

- Have necessary international documents, including your passport, handy and ready for inspection by immigration officials at each border crossing.

- Always keep your camera and other valuables with you at all times.

- If you have a private compartment, keep the door locked and identify anyone wishing to gain access. Know the names of your porters and ask them to identify themselves whenever entering your compartment.

- When in your compartment, be aware that some train thieves will spray chemicals inside to render the occupant(s) unconscious in order to enter and steal valuables. A locked door will at least keep them out.

- If you become suspicious of anyone, or someone bothers you, notify the conductor or other train personnel.

- If you feel you must leave the train temporarily at a stop other than your destination, make certain that you are not left behind.

- An understanding of military time (the so-called 24-hour clock) will make it easier for you to understand the train schedule.

- Make certain you have currency from each of the countries through which you will be traveling. In some lesser-developed countries (and on some trains) it may be advisable to carry your own food and water.

Upon Arrival

- Make certain that you depart from the train at the correct location.

- Use only authorized taxis for transportation to your hotel or other destination.

- Be alert to criminals such as pickpockets, baggage thieves and/or unauthorized taxi drivers/guides.

- If you do not have a hotel reservation, go to the in-station hotel services and reservations desk for help in obtaining a hotel room.

Chapter XI. Driving Abroad

Obtain an International Drivers Permit (IDP). This can be purchased through your AAA Club. Have your passport photos and a completed application. There will be a fee involved. Carry both your IDP and your state driver's license with you at all times.

- Some countries have a minimum and maximum driving age. Check the laws before you drive in any country.

- Always "buckle up". Some countries have penalties for people who violate this law.

- If you rent a car, always purchase the liability insurance. If you do not, this could lead to financial disaster.

- As many countries have different driving rules, obtain a copy of them before you begin driving in that country.

- If the drivers in the country you are visiting drive on the opposite side of the road than in the U.S., practice driving in a less populated area before attempting to drive during the heavy traffic part of the day.

- Be aware of the countryside you will be driving in. Many countries require you to honk your horn before going around a sharp corner or to flash your lights before passing.

- Find out before you start your journey that has the right of way in a traffic circle.

- Always know the route you will be traveling. Have a copy of a good road map, and chart your course before beginning.

- Do not pick up hitchhikers or strangers.

- When entering your vehicle, be aware of your surroundings.

Chapter XII. Personal Conduct Overseas

A hostile or even friendly intelligence organization is always on the lookout for sources who are vulnerable to coercion, addictions, greed or emotional manipulation. To eliminate, or at least diminish, the possibility of your doing something inadvertent that would bring your activities to the special attention of one of these agencies, here are some

DO NOT's to remember:

- DO NOT do anything which might be misconstrued or reflect poorly on your personal judgment, professional demeanor, or embarrassing to you and/or your company.

- DO NOT gossip about character flaws, financial problems, emotional relationships or marital difficulties of anyone working for the company, including yourself. This type of information is eagerly sought after by those who would like to exploit you or another employee.

- DO NOT carry, use or purchase any narcotics, marijuana, or other abused drugs. Some countries have very stringent laws covering the import or use of medications and other substances. If you are using a prescribed medication that contains any narcotic substance or other medication that is subject to abuse, such as amphetamines or tranquilizers, carry a copy of the doctor's prescription for all medications and check your local restrictions and requirements prior to departure. Some countries may require additional documentation/certification from your doctor.

- DO NOT let a friendly ambiance and alcohol override your good sense and capacity when it comes to social drinking. In some countries, heavy drinking in the form of toasting is quite common, and very few westerners can keep up with a local national when it comes to drinking the national brew. An intoxicated or hungover business negotiator could, if they are not careful, prove to be very embarrassing to themselves and expensive to the company. In these situations, prudence is essential.

- DO NOT engage in "Black Market" activities such as the illegal exchange of currency, or the purchase of religious icons or other local antiquities.

- DO NOT accept or deliver letters, packages or anything else from anyone unknown to you. You have no way of knowing what you are carrying and it could result in your being arrested for illegally exporting a prohibited item.

- DO NOT engage in any type of political or religious activity, or carry any political or religious tracts or brochures, or publications likely to be offensive in the host country, such as pornography or mercenary/weapons.

- DO NOT photograph anything that appears to be associated with the military or internal security of the country, including airports, ports, or restricted areas such as military installations. If in doubt, DO NOT.

- DO NOT purchase items that are illegal to import such as endangered species or agricultural products.

Chapter XIII. I've Been Arrested! What Do I Do Now?

Foreign police and intelligence agencies detain persons for a myriad of reasons or for no other reason than suspicion or curiosity. The best advice is to exercise good judgement, be professional in your demeanor and remember the suggestions and hints that are listed in this booklet. But, if you are detained or arrested for some reason, here are some points to remember:

- DO ask to contact the nearest embassy or consulate representing your country. As a citizen of another country, you have this right; but that does not mean that your hosts will allow you to exercise that right. If you are refused or just ignored, continue to make the request periodically until they accede and let you contact your embassy or consulate.

- DO stay calm, maintain your dignity and do not do anything to provoke the arresting officer(s).

- DO NOT admit anything or volunteer any information.

- DO NOT sign anything. Often, part of the detention procedure is to ask or tell the detainee to sign a written report. Decline politely until such time as the document is examined by an attorney or an embassy/consulate representative.

- DO NOT accept anyone on face value. When the representative from the embassy or consulate arrives, request some identification before discussing your situation.

- DO NOT fall for the ruse of helping the ones who are detaining you in return for your release. They can be very imaginative in their proposals on how you can be of assistance to them. Do not sell yourself out by agreeing to anything. If they will not take no for an answer, do not make a firm commitment or sign anything. Tell them that you will think it over and let them know. Once out of their hands, contact the affiliate or your embassy for protection and assistance in getting out of the country.

Chapter XIV. Targeting Recognition

Any person traveling abroad on business should be aware of the fact that they could be targeted by an intelligence agency, security service or, for that matter, a competitor if they are knowledgeable of, or carrying, sensitive or proprietary information. In the course of doing business abroad, there are certain indicators that may occur which should be recognized as potential hazards and indicative of unwarranted interest in your activities. These situations should be closely scrutinized and avoided if at all possible. A few of the most common scenarios that have been utilized by intelligence/security services and have led to successful targeting and acquisition of information are listed below:

- Repeated contacts with a local or third country national who is not involved in your business interests or the purpose of your visit, but as a result of invitations to social or business functions, appears at each function. This individual's demeanor may indicate more than just a passing interest in you and your business activities.

- A close personal social relationship with a foreign national of a hostile host government is often unavoidable for business reasons. In these instances, be cautious and do not allow the relationship to develop any further than the strictly business level.

- Be suspicious of the accidental encounter with an unknown local national who strikes up a conversation and wants to:

- Practice English or other language.

- Talk about your country of origin or your employment.

- Buy you a drink because they have taken a liking to you.

- Talk to you about politics.

- Use a myriad of other excuses to begin a "friendly" relationship.

If any of the above or anything else occurs which just does not ring true, BE SUSPICIOUS!! It may be innocent but, exercise prudence and good judgment.

Chapter XV. Surveillance Recognition

The subject of surveillance is extremely important to anyone conducting business abroad. Surveillance could be indicative of targeting for reasons other than interest by a foreign intelligence or security service. Terrorists and criminals also use surveillance for operational preparation prior to committing other terrorist or criminal acts. It should be noted, however, that the normal business traveler, who only spends a few days in each city and has a low profile, is not really a viable target for terrorists and the risk is very low.

The real terrorist threat to a traveler is that of being at the wrong place at the wrong time and becoming an inadvertent victim of a terrorist act.

Surveillance is an assessment of vulnerabilities in an attempt to determine any information available, from any source, about you or your activities, such as lifestyle or behavior that can be used against you. If the intended target recognizes the fact that he or she is under surveillance, preventive measures can be taken that will hopefully deter further interest. As an example, if the surveillant(s) realizes that he or she has been spotted, then the assumption must be that the operation has been compromised and that the police have been notified or other preventive measures have been taken. On the other hand, if a traveler is being scrutinized by a foreign intelligence or security agency, the surveillance may well continue.

Surveillance takes many forms, from static, such as an observer physically or electronically watching or monitoring your activities in your hotel room or office, to mobile surveillance where the individual being watched is actually followed either on foot or by vehicle.

How do you recognize surveillance? There is only one way: be ALERT to your surroundings. As a traveler, you probably will not be at any one location long enough to know what the norm is in your surroundings, and this puts you at a disadvantage. You will not realize that the person sitting in the car across the street is a stranger and should not be there, whereas a resident would immediately become suspicious.

Be observant and pay attention to your sixth sense. If you get the funny feeling that something is not right or that you are being watched, PAY ATTENTION! That sixth sense is trying to tell you something, and more often than not it will be right.

In any event, report your suspicions or any information to the general manager of the local affiliate or your embassy or consulate just in case something does occur. If there is any question about what actions should be taken, and guidance is not available from the affiliate, contact your embassy or consulate and they will advise you as to what you should do and whether or not the information should be reported to the local authorities. But, the most important thing you should do is making sure that your demeanor is professional and everything you do is above board and not subject to compromise.

If you have reason to believe that you are under surveillance, here is what you should NOT do:

- DO NOT try to slip away or lose the followers as this will probably alert them and belie the fact that you are just a businessperson or tourist going about your business.

- In your hotel room, assume that the room and telephone are being monitored. DO NOT try to play investigator and start looking for electronic listening devices. This again could send the wrong signals to the surveillant. Just make sure that you do not say or do anything in your hotel room that you would not want to see printed on the front page of the New York Times.

Response To Targeting

If you have any reason to believe that you are targeted by an intelligence or security service, there is really only one course of action to follow. Report your suspicions to the affiliate or embassy or consulate and follow their guidance.

Chapter XVI. Hostage Survival

Any traveler could become a hostage. The odds of that happening are extremely low when the number of travelers is compared to the number of people that have actually become a hostage. However, there is always that slim chance that a traveler could end up being in the wrong place at the wrong time. With this in mind, the traveler should make sure that his/her affairs are in order before they travel abroad. Items of particular importance to an individual in a hostage situation are the currentness of an up-to-date will, insurance policy and a power of attorney for the spouse. If these items have been taken care of before departure, the employee will not have to worry about the family's welfare and the hostage can focus all of his/her efforts on the one thing of paramount importance and that is SURVIVAL!!

To survive, travelers should realize that there are certain dynamics involved in a hijacking or a kidnapping, and, to increase their ability to survive, they must understand how these interacting forces affect the end result. Each individual involved in an incident of this type will have an impact on the eventual outcome. One wrong move by either a victim or a perpetrator could easily result in a disaster rather than a peaceful conclusion to the incident.

The first thing that a traveler should remember is that he or she is not the only one that is scared and nervous. Everyone involved is in the same emotional state, including the perpetrators. Fear can trigger a disaster, and it does not take much for some individuals to set off a defensive spate of violence.

Whether it is a demonstration of violence to reinforce a demand or to incite fear in the minds of the hostages, the violence will be motivated by fanaticism and/or fear and that violence will be directed at the person(s) who are perceived to be a threat or a nuisance to the hijackers.

To minimize the possibility of being selected for special attention by the perpetrators and to maximize your ability to survive a hostage situation, here are some guidelines to remember:

Hijacking Survival Guidelines

The physical takeover of the aircraft by the hijackers may be characterized by noise, commotion, and possibly shooting and yelling, or it may be quiet and methodical with little more than an announcement by a crew member. These first few minutes of the hijacking are crucial:

- Stay calm, and encourage others around you to do the same.

- Remember that the hijackers are extremely nervous and are possibly scared.

- Comply with your captor(s) directions.

- If shooting occurs, keep your head down or drop to the floor.

- Remain alert.

Once the takeover of the aircraft has occurred, you may be separated by citizenship, sex, race, etc. Your passport may be confiscated and your carry-on luggage ransacked. The aircraft may be diverted to another country. The hijackers may enter into a negotiation phase, which could last indefinitely, and/or the crew may be forced to fly the aircraft to yet another destination. During this phase passengers may be used as a bargaining tool in negotiations, lives may be threatened, or a number of passengers may be released in exchange for fuel, landing/departure rights, food, etc. This will be the longest phase of the hijacking:

- If you are told to keep your head down or maintain another body position, talk yourself into relaxing into the position; you may need to stay that way for some time.

- Prepare yourself mentally and emotionally for a long ordeal.

- Do not attempt to hide your passport or belongings.

- If addressed by the hijackers, respond in a regulated tone of voice.

- Use your time wisely by observing the characteristics and behavior of the hijackers, mentally attach nicknames to each one and notice their dress, facial features and temperaments.

- If you or a nearby passenger are in need of assistance due to illness or discomfort, solicit the assistance of a crew member first - do not attempt to approach a hijacker unless similar assistance has been rendered by them for other passengers.

- If the hijackers single you out, be responsive but do not volunteer information.

The last phase of the hijacking is resolution, be it by use of a hostage rescue team or resolution through negotiation. In the latter instance, the hijackers may simply surrender to authorities or abandon the aircraft, crew and passengers. In the case of a hostage rescue operation to resolve the hijacking:

- The characteristics of a hostage rescue force introduction into the aircraft will be similar to the hijacker's takeover - noise, chaos, possibly shooting - the rescue force is re-taking control of the aircraft.

- If you hear shots fired inside or outside the aircraft, immediately take a protective position - put your head down or drop to the floor.

- If instructed by a rescue force to move, do so quickly, putting your hands up in the air or behind your head; make no sudden movements.

- If fire or smoke appears, attempt to get emergency exits open, and use the inflatable slides or exit onto the wing.

- Once you are on the tarmac, follow the instructions of the rescue force or local authorities; if neither are there to guide you, move as quickly as possible away from the aircraft and eventually move towards the terminal or control tower area.

- Expect to be treated as a hijacker or co-conspirator by the rescue force; initially you will be treated roughly until it is determined by the rescue force that you are not part of the hijacking team.

- Cooperate with local authorities and members of the U.S. Embassy, Consulate or other U.S. agencies in relating information about the hijacking.

- Onward travel and contact with family members will be arranged by U.S. authorities as soon as possible.

Chapter XVII. Kidnapping Survival Guidelines

Kidnapping can take place in public areas where someone may quietly force you, by gunpoint, into a vehicle. They can also take place at a hotel or residence, again by using a weapon to force your cooperation in leaving the premises and entering a vehicle. The initial phase of kidnapping is a critical one because it provides one of the best opportunities to escape.

- If you are in a public area at the time of abduction, make as much commotion as possible to draw attention to the situation.

- If the abduction takes place at your hotel room, make noise, attempt to arouse the suspicion or concern of hotel employees or of those in neighboring rooms - minimally, the fact that an abduction has taken place will be brought to the attention of authorities and the process of notification and search can begin. Otherwise, it could be hours or days before your absence is reported.

- Once you have been forced into a vehicle, you may be blindfolded, physically attacked (to cause unconsciousness), drugged, or forced to lie face down on the floor of the vehicle. In some instances, hostages have been forced into trunks or specially built compartments for transporting contraband.

- Do not struggle in your confined state; calm yourself mentally, concentrate on surviving.

- Employ your mind by attempting to visualize the route being taken, take note of turns, street noise, smells, etc. Try to keep track of the amount of time spent between points.

- Once you have arrived at your destination, you may be placed in a temporary holding area before being moved again to a more permanent detention site. If you are interrogated:

- Retain a sense of pride but be cooperative.

- Divulge only information that cannot be used against you.

- Do not antagonize your interrogator with obstinate behavior.

- Concentrate on surviving; if you are to be used as a bargaining tool or to obtain ransom, you will be kept alive.

After reaching what you may presume to be your permanent detention site (you may be moved several more times), quickly settle into the situation:

- Be observant - Notice the details of the room, the sounds of activity in the building and determine the layout of the building by studying what is visible to you. Listen for sounds through walls, windows or out in the streets, and try to distinguish between smells.

- Stay mentally active by memorizing the aforementioned details. Exercise your memory and practice retention.

- Keep track of time. Devise a way to track the day, date and the time, and use it to devise a daily schedule of activities for yourself.

- Know your captors. Memorize their schedule, look for patterns of behavior to be used to your advantage, and identify weaknesses or vulnerabilities.

- Use all of the above information to seek opportunities to escape.

- Remain cooperative. Attempt to establish rapport with your captors or guards. Once a level of communication is achieved, try asking for items that will increase your personal comfort. Make them aware of your needs.

- Stay physically active even if your movement is extremely limited. Use isometric and flexing exercises to keep your muscles toned.

- If you detect the presence of other hostages in the same building, devise ways to communicate.

- DO NOT be uncooperative, antagonistic, or hostile towards your captors. It is a fact that hostages who display this type of behavior are kept captive longer or are singled out for torture or punishment.

- Watch for signs of Stockholm Syndrome, which occurs when the captive, due to the close proximity and the constant pressures involved, begins to relate to, and empathize with, the captors. In some cases, this relationship has resulted in the hostage become empathetic to the point that he/she actively participates in the activities of the group. You should attempt to establish a friendly rapport with your captors, but maintain your personal dignity and do not compromise your integrity.

- If you are able to escape, attempt to get first to a U.S. Embassy or Consulate to seek protection. If you cannot reach either, go to a host government or friendly government entity.

Chapter XVIII. Conclusion

It is no wonder that most U.S. business people consider business travel hard work - and one of the most stressful aspects of their job. The running, waiting, and anxiety associated with travel can take its toll on the mind and body. Add an unfamiliar location, a foreign language, and a different culture to the situation and you have the potential for all sorts of problems.

As pointed out in this publication, the keys to safe travel are planning and sound security practices. Proper planning ensures your logistical plan is in place and you have the necessary background information to support your itinerary. Incorporating sound security practices into your travel routine will reduce the likelihood of problems. Together, these keys allow you to get on with the real purpose of your trip.

The Overseas Security Advisory Council's Travel Safety Reference Guide

Introduction

Globalization has made overseas travel – be it for business, academia, charity, personal, or mission work – quite common. International travelers are exposed to many new experiences and phenomena and among these, certain risks. This guide offers international travelers information, tactics, techniques, and procedures to mitigate risks inherent to international travel.

OSAC acknowledges that every destination is unique and that no one resource can address all eventualities. Therefore, we have developed this reference in coordination with our constituents to inform the private sector of best practices for personnel safety abroad. The risks of international travel are no longer just tied to local or transnational crime. It is our hope that the enclosed recommendations will both encourage individuals to seek overseas opportunities and provide greater comfort and confidence for those traveling internationally.

Pre-Departure

Know Before You Go

- Register with the U.S. State Department's Smart Traveler Enrollment Program (STEP).
- Review the U.S. State Department's country specific information and OSAC's country crime and safety reports.
- Do your homework. Visit country-specific websites for important information on your destination country.
- Understand the laws and currency exchange rates in your destination country.
- Be culturally aware; learn a few common phrases in the local language and the basics of the cultural values and norms.
- Get a map and study it. Identify potential hazards and safe havens; learn several routes to key places you will be staying/living/visiting.

Packing

- Pack your luggage wisely. Make sure to place any prohibited materials (scissors, files, other sharp objects) in your check-in luggage.
- Be sure to pack 2-3 day "survival items" in your carry-on bag. This includes: medicines

and toiletries, an extra change of clothes (including undergarments), important documents, drinking water, snacks (e.g., Powerbars), and anything else you may want.
- Do not display company or other identifying logos on luggage. Place your pertinent con-tact information in a visible place inside each piece of luggage.
- Do not openly display your name tags on your luggage. Include only your name and contact number on your tags, and keep them covered or turn the paper over and write "see other side."
- Get a plain cover for your passport.
- Make out a will.
- Consider a privacy act waiver.
- Leave travel itinerary and contact information with family or friends; do not otherwise disclose.
- Consider getting a telephone calling card and a GSM (tri-band or "world") cellular phone that allows access to most local cellular systems (and provides a single contact number). Depending on your situation, you may want to purchase a local phone or SIM card in country.
- Take out property insurance on necessary equipment (cameras, binoculars, laptops, etc.).

- Consider securing a new credit card with a low credit limit separate from existing credit cards; in the event of theft, your personal accounts will not be compromised.
- Notify your credit card company of your intent to travel; confirm credit limit and availability.

Health

- Make sure health insurance covers foreign medical providers and medical evacuation expenses.
- Take an extra pair of glasses; depending on the destination, contact lenses can be problematic.
- Visit a travel clinic, inform them of destination(s), and get any needed inoculations and medications.
- Get a dental cleaning and checkup if you had not recently had one.
- Prep and pack a travel med kit; some items you may want to include:
    - Anti-diarrheal medication
    - Antibiotics
    - Anti-malaria (if applicable)
    - Antihistamine and decongestant
    - Antacid and laxative
    - Anti-fungal/anti-bacterial and hydrocortisone cream

- Anti-bacterial hand wipes/ hand sanitizer
- Pain reliever/fever reducer, sleep aid
- Gauze, bandages, and medical tape
- Insect repellant with DEET 35%
- Shaving razor, tweezers, manicure kits
- Sunscreen and aloe
- Thermometer

During Your Trip

Awareness

Situational Awareness is very important domestically but becomes critically important overseas in unfamiliar environments. Keep your head up, eyes and ears open, and listen to your intuition! Situational awareness can and should be practiced and will improve the more you do so. Focus on seeing and remembering everything around you. It will seem extremely arduous and time-consuming at first but will become increasingly easier as time passes and proficiency is gained. Your goal should be for these efforts to become habitual and completed subconsciously. Some important practices are:

- Trust your instinct; if a place does not feel right, move to a safer location – immediately.

- Assess your emotional and physical strengths and limitations.
- Be attentive to how others perceive you; behave in an unprovocative manner that discourages un-wanted attention.
- Familiarize yourself with your neighborhood and work environment.
- Use common sense. Beware of EVERYONE, including pickpockets, scam artists, etc.
- Remove name tags or convention badges when outside the venue.
- Pay attention to local media for any activities or events that might affect you.
- Be aware of surroundings, including the people, cars, and alleys nearby.
- Keep alert to potential trouble, and choose to avoid when possible. Trust your instincts.
- Educate yourself of any pending events (elections, demonstrations, anniversaries) that may cause civil disturbance, and avoid unnecessary risks.
- Establish a support network among your colleagues and when possible, embassy personnel.
- Inform yourself of the availability and reliability of local support services (police, security, medical, emergency, fire).

- Confirm (with your embassy) the procedures for you and your family in the event of a crisis or evacuation.
- Politely decline offers of food or drink from strangers.
- Accept beverages only in sealed containers; make sure there has been no tampering.

Personal Conduct

You can dress, behave, and move about in a manner that is respectful of local custom, but rest assured, YOU WILL NOT BLEND IN. Remember that whenever you travel anywhere, whether you realize it or not, you are representing yourself, your family, your organization, and your country. Your behavior and actions will be applied as a positive or negative impression of all that you represent. In many cultures, this will essentially make or break your ability to successfully function and interact in another culture. Always keep in mind the following:

- Behave maturely and in a manner befitting your status in the local society; insist on being treated with respect.
- Dress in a manner that is inoffensive to local cultural norms.
- Avoid clothing that shows your nationality or political views.

- Establish personal boundaries and act to protect them.
- Exercise additional caution when carrying and displaying valuable possessions (jewelry, phone, sun-glasses, camera, etc.); what may be a simple, even disposable item to you, may be a sign of extreme affluence to another.
- Vary your patterns of life/behavior to be less predictable.
- Divide money among several pockets; if you carry a wallet, carry it in a front pocket.
- If you carry a purse, carry it close to your body. Do not set it down or leave it unattended.
- Take a patient and calm approach to ambiguity and conflict.
- Radiate confidence while walking in public places.
- Do not expect privacy, anywhere.
- Do not discuss personal, professional, or financial issues of your group or yourself; these can be used to exploit you and your group.
- Be cool when facing confrontation; focus on de-escalation and escape.
- Respect local sensitivities to photographing/videotaping, especially at airports, police, and government facilities.
- Carry required official identification with you at all times.

- Report any security incidents to your embassy or consulate (who will advise you of options including reporting to local authorities, prosecution, corrective measures, etc.).
- Maintain a low profile, especially in places where there may be hostility toward foreigners and/or citizens of your country; do not seek publicity.
- Avoid public expressions about local politics, religion, and other sensitive topics.
- Avoid being out alone late at night or after curfew.
- Stay alert.
- Be unpredictable.
- Carry yourself with confidence.
- Be aware of distractions.
- Watch for surveillance. If you see the same person/vehicle twice, it could be surveillance; if you see it three times, it probably is surveillance.

Electronics Security

- First and foremost: if you don't NEED it, don't bring it!
- If you need to bring a laptop and/or phone and have "clean" ones available, use them.

- Back up and then wipe (sanitize) your laptop, phone, and any other electronics to ensure that no sensitive or personal data is on them while traveling.
- Carry laptop in a protective sleeve in a backpack/purse/bag that does not shout "there's a computer in here."
- DO NOT EXPECT PRIVACY, ANYWHERE.
- Do not leave your electronic devices unattended.
- Do not use local computers to connect to your organization's secure network.
- Clear your temporary files, to include your temporary internet files, browser history, caches, and cookies after each use.
- Consider opening a new e-mail account (Gmail, Yahoo, Hotmail, AOL, etc.) for use during your trip.
- Ensure you update your computer's security software (antivirus, firewall, etc.) and download any out-standing security patches for your operating system and key programs.
- Upon return, change all of your passwords for devices and accounts (including voicemail) used while traveling.

Logistics

Air Travel

Air travel can be incredibly convenient and frustrating at the same time. While traveling you are extremely vulnerable and must bear this in mind that a distracted individual is a prime target for all kinds of nefarious actions. You must control what you can and readily adapt to, as well as what you cannot (i.e., flight schedules/delays and time to clear security). Here are some key considerations:

- Wear comfortable, loose fitting clothing.
- Arrive at the airport in plenty of time (1.5 – 2 hours before departure).
- Move through passenger security immediately after ticketing and locate your departure gate.
- Stay with your bags at all times.
- Set your watch to local time at destination upon take off.
- Be careful about how much of your personal/business information you share with fellow passengers; they are still strangers.
- Limit intake of alcohol in flight, and drink plenty of water to counteract "jet lag". This will help limit stress and increase alertness.
- If possible, pre-arrange transport from the airport to your hotel. Consider paying the

additional room rate for a hotel that provides shuttle service to and from the airport.
- Have your immigration and customs documents in order and available. A durable folder secured by a buckle or elastic band may be useful.

Ground Travel

Ground travel poses several risks to the traveler. Not only are you more vulnerable, but many places do not have the traffic laws, enforcement, infrastructure, or assistance that you are accustomed to. Be prepared. You will be in an unfamiliar environment and may have to contend with, among other things, dangerous road conditions; untrained or unlicensed drivers; drivers operating under the influence of alcohol and/or narcotics; vehicles that are poorly maintained and therefore hazardous, police and/or criminal checkpoints or roadblocks, and others with malicious intentions. Some recommendations for ground travel are:

- Use a common vehicle model (local taxis may be a good indicator). If you rent, remove any markings that identify vehicle as a rental.
- If you have to drive, always leave a path for escape when you stop (at a light, stop sign, cross-walk, etc.).

- Park in a manner that expedites your departure.
- Carry a cell phone, first aid kit, maps, flashlight, and official documents in your vehicle.
- Keep the vehicle windows rolled up and the doors locked.
- Use the seat belts.
- Be alert to scam artists and carjackers while stopped in traffic.
- Understand the proper local procedures should you be involved in or witness a traffic accident. In some locales, stopping for an accident can put your life at risk.
- Only take official, licensed taxis; note the license plate number of taxi and write it down.
- Avoid getting into a taxi already occupied by others. If necessary, pay extra for a single fare. Negotiate a price before getting in taxi. Have money ready to pay in appropriate denominations.
- Take a seat on a bus or train that allows you to observe fellow passengers but does not preclude options to change seats if necessary.

Lodging

At the Hotel

- For most destinations you travel to (in addition to being an obvious foreigner), you will be considered wealthy and a prime target. You should not consider a hotel a complete safe haven, there are still many threats and you are potentially very vulnerable at them. Some important considerations:
- Use reputable hotels, hostels, or boarding houses; your safety is worth any added cost.
- Remind hotel staff to not give out your room number.
- Meet visitors in the lobby; avoid entertaining strangers in your room.
- Take a walk around the hotel facilities to familiarize yourself with your environment. Are hotel personnel located on each floor? Are they in uniform? Do they display any identification? Who else has access to your floor?
- Ensure the phone in your room works. Call the front desk.
- Inspect the room carefully; look under the bed, in the showers and closets.
- Ensure door and window locks are working. Do not forget the sliding glass door, if the room has one.

- Ensure the door has a peephole and chain lock.
- Avoid ground floor rooms at the hotel. Third through fifth floors are normally desirable (harder to break into, but still accessible to firefighting equipment – where available).
- Read the safety instructions in your hotel room. Familiarize yourself with hotel emergency exits and fire extinguishers.
- Count the doors between your room and nearest emergency exit (in case of fire or blackout). Re-hearse your escape plan.
- Keep all hotel doors locked with a dead bolt or chain at all times (do not forget the sliding glass door and windows).
- Consider traveling with a rubber door stop, smoke detector, and motion detector.
- Identify your visitor before you open the door.
- If you doubt room delivery, check with the front desk before opening the door.
- If you are out of your room, leave television/radio on at high volume. Place a "do not disturb" sign outside door.
- Do not leave sensitive documents or valuables visible and unattended in the room.
- Keep your laptop out of sight, in a safe, or in a locked suitcase. You may wish to use a laptop cable lock to secure your laptop to a window frame or bathroom plumbing.

- Keep your room number to yourself. If your room key is numbered or has your room number on a key holder, keep it out of sight. If a hotel clerk announces your room number loud enough for others to hear, ask for a new room.
- If you leave the hotel, carry the hotel business card with you; it may come in handy with a taxi driver who does not speak your language.

Residential

When residing overseas, it is critically important to understand the threat environment in which you will be living. Take the time to reach out to the resources available, including security professionals in your organization, the local embassy or consulate, and the appropriate crime and safety reports. Here are some security measures you might want to consider:

- Avoid housing on single-entry streets with a dead end or cul-de-sac.
- Housing near multiple intersections can be beneficial.
- Ensure the sound, secure structure of your residence.
- Strictly control access to and distribution of keys.

- Install adequate lighting, window grilles, alarm systems, and perimeter walls as necessary.
- Establish access procedures for strangers and visitors.
- Hire trained guards and night patrols; periodically check-up on guards.
- Set-up a safe room in your house; consider adding additional locks
- Establish rapport with neighbors. Is there a "neighborhood watch" program?
- Seek guidance from local colleagues or expatriates who have insight into local housing arrangements.
- Ensure adequate communications (telephone, radio, cell phone) with local colleagues, authorities, and your Embassy.
- Install a back-up generator and/or solar panels.
- Set aside emergency supplies (food, water, medicine, fuel, etc.).
- Install smoke detectors, fire extinguishers, and carbon monoxide monitors, as appropriate.
- Avoid sleeping with the windows open or unlocked.
- Speak on the phone inside, somewhere that is and away from windows (through which you can be seen and heard).

- Ensure all windows have treatments that can prevent external observation.
- Lock up items, such as ladders and hand-tools, which could be used to facilitate forced entry.
- Store emergency funds in multiple places around the house.
- Keep a "go-bag" with clothes, water, and food (Powerbars, etc.) for three days packed and ready at all times. Keep copies of important documents and some emergency funds with the bag. Keep other necessary items (medications, etc.) in a centralized place for easy placement into bag. Key items include:
    - Documentation
    - Copies of all key documentation
    - Passport and/or national ID
    - Driver's License
    - Health Insurance Card
    - Communication
    - Mobile phone – including a charger and extra battery
    - Work and emergency contact lists
    - Satellite Phone (if available)
    - GPS devise (if available)
    - Food and water
    - Water bottle
    - Purification tablets
    - Energy bars / dried fruit / nuts

- Other essentials
- Cash (USD and local currency)
- Full change of clothing
- Rain jacket
- Sweater
- Walking shoes or boots (with heel and closed toe)
- Insect repellant
- Matches (ideally windproof and waterproof)
- Flashlight (with extra batteries)
- Medical/first aid kit
- Sun screen
- Sunglasses
- Toiletries
- Toilet paper
- Extended items
- Sleeping bag or blanket
- Mosquito net

Preparation for the "what if" scenarios

If You Become a Victim

Despite all of your efforts to reduce exposure to risks and to avoid threats, you may still become the victim of a crime or critical event. Following are some general response strategies:

- Remain calm and alert.
- Carefully note details of the environment around you (license plate number, distinguishing features, accents, clothing, etc.).
- First, try to defuse the situation. Culturally appropriate greetings or humor may reduce tensions.
- If an assailant demands property, give it up.
- You can create a timely diversion by tossing your wallet, watch, etc. to the ground in the opposite direction you choose to flee.
- Against overwhelming odds (weapons, multiple assailants) try reasoning, cajoling, begging, or any psychological ploy.
- If someone tries to grab you, make a scene and fight; kick, punch, claw, scratch, and grab as if your life depends on it, it very well could.
- If you feel your life is endangered and you decide to physically resist, commit to the decision with every fiber of your being; turn fear into fury.
- Report any incident your embassy.
- Seek support for post-traumatic stress (even if you exhibit no symptoms).

Hijacking/Kidnapping

You may be targeted for kidnapping. As discussed previously, when traveling, you represent your-self, your family, your organization, and your homeland (or perceived homeland). You may be targeted due to any of these affiliations, or you may simply just end up in the wrong place at the wrong time. Because abduction situations vary greatly, the following considerations should be applied based on one's best judgment at the time:

- Know the "ransom" policy of your government. The United States of America will not pay a ransom.
- The greatest risk of physical harm exists at the point of capture and during a rescue attempt or upon release.
- If you are going to resist at the point of capture, do so as if your life depends on it; it most probably does.
- Remain calm and alert; exert control on your emotions and behavior.
- Humanize yourself, quickly and continually.
- Be passively cooperative, but maintain your dignity.
- Assume an inconspicuous posture and avoid direct eye contact with captors.
- Avoid resistance, belligerence, or threatening movements.

- Make reasonable, low-key requests for personal comforts (bathroom breaks, a blanket, exercise, books to read, etc.)
- If questioned, keep answers short; volunteer nothing.
- As a captive situation draws out, try to establish some rapport with your captors.
- Avoid discussing contentious issues (politics, religion, ethnicity, etc.)
- Establish a daily regimen to maintain your body physically and mentally.
- Eat what your captors provide. Avoid alcohol.
- Keep a positive, hopeful attitude.
- Attempt to escape only after weighing the risks and when you are certain to succeed.

11 Best Practices for Crisis Preparedness

At the 2021 OSAC Annual Briefing, Ambassador Michele Sison, now Assistant Secretary of State for International Organization Affairs participated in a panel on amorphous threats. During the panel, she gave an informative list all security managers should take while preparing for the possibility of insecurity abroad. Although the exact responses to a terror attack may differ from that of a kidnapping, a protest that has turned violent, a natural disaster, or any other type of potentially dangerous situation, the steps Amb. Sison laid out are ideal boxes for security managers of any size organization to check when preparing for emergencies involving their personnel, facilities, or operations. The overarching themes are preparation and communication. After all, many times the most mundane of administrative actions and the simplest personal interactions can mean the most in a time of crisis.

Preparation

1. Physical Accountability

It may sound exceedingly simple, but do you know where your people are? Sure, you know where your employees work, and you might know where they are while they're traveling on business. But what about after work, on weekends, on personal trips away. Do you have a personnel locator system? Especially for employees abroad, this can be of paramount importance. In the case of an emergency, you don't want to have to worry about trying to account for people who aren't in an affected location. Develop and maintain a system to account for the whereabouts of your people, and ensure they keep the system up to date. Everyone for whom you are responsible while they are abroad should at least tell you every time they are away from their station; you decide where that distance threshold should stand.

2. Practice Makes Perfect

Drills are so important. We run fire drills in elementary school, but do we run drills for more complicated emergencies in a professional setting? Practice makes perfect, and emergency drills are no different. Think about all the potential emergencies that might affect your workplace: natural disasters, criminal issues, terror attacks, utility failures, personnel medical emergencies. Make sure the drills focus on differences between the emergencies and account for all possibilities based on local variables; fire drills should look and feel different than active shooter drills. Develop realistic and simple reaction plans, and run regular and mandatory drills with your entire staff; everyone from new hires to the CEO needs to participate, and nobody should know when they might happen.

3. Temporary Hideouts

Think about those various emergencies, and figure out how best to incorporate safe haven locations in your facilities and in your personnel's homes. This doesn't have to mean bullet-proof safe rooms—though it could! Is your housing in a flood-prone region? Make sure there is easy access to a higher story. Do your offices have windowless rooms with reinforced doors in case of an active shooter or other intruder? And is there a phone in that room? You might already walk around your facility looking for potential security vulnerabilities, but make sure you take housing into account as well, especially if you have a duty of care to your international staff.

4. Avoid Predictability

By now, avoiding time and place predictability should be a standard SOP for anyone in an environment prone to insecurity, right? But we all tend to fall into routines, and switching things up isn't easy. While managers can ask personnel to maintain personal security by using different routes and visiting different locations, what can organizations do to build that into their overall plans? How about staggering work schedules so there aren't bottlenecks at the exits? How about offering remote work so employees don't have to commute through a potentially problematic environment every day? Avoiding time/place predictability isn't just about physical security, either. Just as a terrorist might take advantage of predictability, so would someone intent on stealing information from someone who uses the same café wi-fi every morning or takes a work call on a stroll through the same park every afternoon.

5. Take Advantage of Available Resources

The U.S. Government—and other governments around the world—has prioritized the safety and security of its nationals abroad. But even the best programs need participation to be effective! Security managers need to impress on their international staff the importance of registering with programs like the Smart Traveler Enrollment Program (STEP), which gives U.S. nationals abroad instant notification of security alerts from the nearest U.S. embassy or consulate. Managers themselves should register as OSAC members to get access to the most relevant and timely security information, not to mention an office of security analysts and program managers ready to help. While your third-country national employees' home governments might have programs like STEP, they should at least have the emergency contact information for their nearest embassy or consulate programmed into their phones.

6. Prepare for the Extreme

Drawdowns and evacuations can be fraught processes for even the most prepared institutions, but they can be especially difficult for personnel who must uproot their lives—and possibly those of their families—to leave their location in an instant. Once you draw up organizational tripwires and SOPs, ensure you communicate them effectively to your personnel. Explain to locally employed staff how they are (or might not be) involved. What happens to pets during an immediate evacuation? Do you have a travel agency located outside of the country available to ticket passengers to leave on short notice, in case insecurity makes domestic ticketing impossible? Will staff be reimbursed if they have to pay their own way out due to organizational mandate (or if they choose to do so despite the lack of one)? Have you prepared for contingencies by securing visas for neighboring countries in case the best way out of an emergency is a road convoy?

Communication

7. Reach Your Personnel...

Sometimes, old-school solutions stick around because nothing better has come along to supplant them. There may be plenty of technology that appears to make the old phone tree system obsolete—think email distribution lists and listservs, robo-calls, or telephone apps—but often these solutions to information sharing dilemmas have single points of failure. What if the electricity or internet goes out? What if the person charged with starting the whole process is out of commission? Don't make one person or one program account for everyone. Institute a simple phone tree to get the word out, especially in areas prone to technology/utility failure, and don't forget to program numbers into your cell phones. Even when phone trees don't work, it's easy to work backwards to find out where the break in the chain exists.

8. ... And Their Families

You've drilled plans with your employees, you've noted where your employees are traveling, you've updated them on the latest threats. But are you talking to their family members? Don't forget that many of your personnel might be in-country with their families, who may have very different experiences than your employees. A spouse might work for a local organization, which might not see security the same as an international organization would; will they know where to evacuate in case of emergency weather conditions? Kids going to school might experience insecurity while their school bus is en route, like protests that stop traffic; do they know what to do in case a march turns violent? Develop materials for family members of various ages and situations, and offer them not only to your international employees, but to your local staff as well.

9. Relationships = Information

What is your relationship with local law enforcement? (You do have a relationship with local law enforcement, right?) Even in an area with a capable and responsible police force, it can only help to have a working relationship with the professionals that might be your first line of defense if things go wrong. Meet with local police officers and other relevant agencies to explain your situation, your potential needs, and your security concerns. Explain to them why your presence is beneficial for the community; find out if you need to supplement their capabilities with some (more) of your own. Set up a healthy line of communication between your shop and the local police so they can easily contact you when the security environment is taking a turn for the worse. And make sure your communication goes two ways: report incidents, lend a hand when you can, and be a good neighbor.

10. Keep Your Ears to the Ground

Police know the beat, but so do civilians. What other ways are there for you to find out local security information? Set up social media alerts hooked to local sources and tagged for local issues. Create wider searches for overall environmental shifts, but personalize searches to keep abreast of more granular changes in the neighborhoods around your facilities and lodging. Don't overlook social and traditional media sources in a local language, and make sure you have a local employee on your staff with their ears to the ground. You may not be the very first to know when the winds shift, but you certainly don't want to be the last.

11. Alternative Methods of Communication

How do you keep in touch with your staff? Do you call them on their cell phone, or text them? Or do you email them, or maybe use WhatsApp or Twitter? Great! You likely know the best way to get information to your people. But consider changing all of those ORs into ANDs! Keep current lists of phone numbers, addresses, work and personal email addresses, and anything else that will help you reach your personnel in an emergency. And what if an emergency hits when someone has forgotten to charge their phone, or mobile service is cut? Think about two-way radios, satellite phones – and even land lines -- as secondary or tertiary ways to get information in or out during an emergency. Redundant communications are incredibly important if a storm knocks out cell towers, if an app's servers go down, or if a local government disables certain forms of communication. But they could also be good if your employee switches cell carriers (and phone numbers) without remembering to tell the office. Redundant communications will not only help your emergency planning but your administrative messaging as well.

Security Guidelines for American Families Living Abroad

Effective security precautions require a continuous and conscious awareness of your environment. This is especially true when living in a foreign country where it will be necessary to adapt to new cultures, customs, and laws, which, in most instances, are very different than those to which Americans are accustomed in the United States.

Security precautions not only lessen your vulnerability to criminal and terrorist acts, but greatly facilitate the assistance the U. S. Government can render, where possible, to all Americans and their families living abroad.

The Council recognizes that many American organizations, especially the larger ones, employ numerous foreign nationals at locations abroad. It would be presumptuous of the Council to suggest security guidelines from an American perspective to these foreign nationals in their native land. For this reason, these security guidelines are primarily for American citizens living abroad.

Chapter I. Introduction

This booklet is a compilation of diverse security measures for consideration by American private sector employees and their families living and working outside the United States. Obviously, the implementation of security precautions described herein should be consistent with the level of risk currently existing in the foreign country of residence.

Diverse political climates, local laws and customs, and a wide range of other variables make it impossible to apply standard security precautions worldwide.

Levels of risk can change very rapidly, sometimes overnight, triggered by internal or external incidents or circumstances. It is advisable, therefore, to monitor continually the political climate and other factors which may impact the level of risk. Remember that establishing a family residence abroad requires much more security planning than a short-term visit to a foreign country for business or pleasure.

It is essential that security precautions be kept under constant review so that they may be adapted to respond effectively to any changes in the level of risk. An inflexible security posture would be indicative of a disregard for the climate of risk and will almost certainly result in a lack of preparedness.

Chapter II. Preliminary Residential Security Planning

Need for Planning

Begin to develop a tentative Residential Security Plan for yourself and all members of your family before leaving the U.S. This is essential in providing you the guidelines for selecting your future home and determining where your children will go to school, the type of car you will buy, the kind of clothing you will wear (and not wear) and the information required to live securely in your forthcoming overseas location.

Your Residential Security Plan should progress from a tentative to an active plan. The latter, however, is not to be considered final because you should keep it under continuing review and update it regularly as circumstances dictate.

Primary Concept - Low Profile

A single concept, more than any other, should permeate all planning activities, namely keep a low profile. In other words, do not draw attention to yourself as an American by driving a big American car, having American publications delivered to residential mail box or doorsteps, or having displays at your residence which will identify you as an

American. Common sense and knowledge of local cultures and mores must guide you to what extent you should blend into local environs. Appearing to "go native" may subject you to ridicule and be counter-productive in keeping a low profile.

Keeping a low profile also entails staying away from civil disturbances, protesters and mobs, and not visiting or, if possible, traversing high-risk areas.

Information Required, and Where to Get It

- To keep a low profile and to know what pitfalls must be avoided, you need to inform yourself about your new location if you are to live safely there. Much professional help is available for the family moving overseas. Major multinational corporations have large international departments and corporate security departments that may serve as valuable resources for Residential Security Planning. Libraries have an abundance of current reference materials on working and living abroad.

- Obtain a current political profile of the country to which you will be moving to aid you in assessing the level of risk. Corporate Security Directors of large multinational companies can identify a number of commercial organizations, which publish political profiles of most countries as well as periodic updates.

- You and your family should study the culture and customs of the country. Use library sources and reference works.

Chapter III. Assessing the Level of Risk at Overseas Location

Two factors must be taken into consideration when evaluating the seriousness of the personal risk to you and your family when contemplating a move abroad:

- A risk assessment of the location to which you will be moving.

- The profile of the company for which you work. Highly visible defense contractors may not be welcome in some parts of the world.

The threat assessment designators below were formulated by the Department of State Threat Analysis Division in the Diplomatic Security Service. The assessments are reevaluated by the Department of State quarterly with new levels being assigned when and where appropriate.

This assessment information is available to the business community through the Regional Security

Officer (RSO) at the U.S. Embassy. The level assigned to a particular country is the result of the political/terrorist/criminal environment in that country.

- High - The threat is serious and forced entries and assaults on residents are common or an active terrorist threat exists.

- Medium - The threat is moderate with forced entries and some assaults on residents occurring, or the area has potential for terrorist activity.

- Low - The threat is minimal and forced entry of residences and assault of occupants is not common. There is no known terrorist threat.

Chapter IV. Location of the Residence

Finding a Safe Neighborhood

The first step in the residence selection process should be choosing a safe neighborhood. The local police, the RSO or Post Security Officer (PSO) at the nearest U.S. diplomatic post, i.e., Embassy or Consulate, other American residents, and other sources, will facilitate this process.

Street Conditions

During the neighborhood selection process, particular attention should be paid to the condition of the streets, e.g., paved or unpaved, maintenance condition, wide or narrow, one-way or two-way traffic (two-way is preferred). Parked and/or double-parked vehicles could impede access to, or egress from, the residence. Density of pedestrian traffic could create security hazards. Dense vehicular and/or pedestrian traffic facilitates retention of anonymity of criminals and surveillants.

Note the overall security precautions that are taken in the neighborhood, such as barred windows, security fences, extensive lighting, large dogs, and security guards. Such visible precautions may indicate a high level of security awareness or a high crime area. Ensure you properly interpret reasons for it by checking the crime levels with RSO or local police.

Susceptibility to Clandestine Approach

You should examine the quality of lighting at night time to determine whether it is sufficient to illuminate the entrance to homes in the area. At the very least it should suffice to deter someone from lurking undetected in adjacent areas. Also, you should assure that there are no trees or shrubbery on the grounds which provide cover for a clandestine approach and concealment, or that you may remove them if you move in.

Access Routes

Statistics of kidnappings and assassinations have shown that the vast majority occur close to the residence when the victim is leaving or returning home. Therefore, it is essential that access routes to and from the residence provide sufficient alternatives which do not lock you into predictable patterns. Specifically, it is essential that dead-end streets or narrow one-way streets be avoided. If possible, your residence also should afford more than one point of entrance/exit.

Parking

Underground parking, unless tightly controlled, should be avoided particularly in high threat areas and in multi-story buildings. Ideally, a garage that can be locked is the most suitable means of securing vehicles at single family dwellings. Carports and driveways within fenced or guarded areas will also normally suffice. Parking the car on the street should be avoided.

Nearby Friends

You may want to consider residences located near friends or co-workers. This could enable you to car pool, especially during periods of high stress and to have them share with you any observations of suspicious activities in the neighborhood.

Chapter V. Selection of Residence

Apartment vs Single Dwelling

Given a choice between apartment or single dwelling living, an apartment offers greater protection against criminal intrusion. An apartment, especially one above the second floor, presents a more difficult target, provides the tenant some degree of anonymity, provides the benefit of close neighbors, and is almost always easier and less expensive to modify with security hardware. In the event of an emergency and loss of communications, neighbors can often be relied upon to come to another tenant's assistance. At the very least, they can notify the authorities.

Apartment Pros and Cons

Apartments on the first or second floors should be avoided because of their immediate and easy accessibility from the street level or from tree tops of large vehicles, or porch roofs. Foreign objects can easily be introduced to first and second floor apartments from the outside area accessible to the public.

Although an apartment above the second or third floor is preferred, do not select apartments on floors above the fire fighting and rescue capabilities of the local fire department. Even the most sophisticated fire and rescue equipment has limitations. In most countries it would be well not to live above the seventh floor.

It is important that access to the lobby of the apartment building be tightly controlled by a doorman or an electronic system such as card key readers or CCTV.

Surveillance of a particular target is sometimes more difficult in an apartment building because of multiple tenants.

Single Dwelling Pros and Cons

The private or single dwelling allows the occupant greater opportunity to establish more rigid access control to the property. However, since single dwelling residences are seldom designed or built with security as a major consideration, it is usually more difficult to achieve good security.

Safe Haven Suitability

In certain areas where an active terrorist threat exists or there is a serious crime threat with forced entries and assaults on residents being common, it may be prudent to consider the need for a safe haven in any residence that may be selected, i.e. a place in a residence which can serve as an area where occupants may take refuge for short periods of time until help arrives.

If it is determined that there is a need for a safe haven, this factor should be included in the selection of a residence. Then the type, layout and construction of a residence should be assessed to decide whether it lends itself to constructing such an area.

A basic requirement for a safe haven is that it be furnished with a substantial door equipped with a door viewer or with a grill gate. The door or gate should be equipped with a strong deadbolt lock. (NOTE: A "substantial" door is made of material which is strong enough to prevent someone from breaking through by kicking, throwing body weight against it, or striking it with a heavy item such as a rock or hammer. A door below this standard may suffice if it is used with a good quality grill gate.)

The safe haven area also should be equipped with reliable communications and accessible windows/openings should be secured against forced entry. Furthermore, a desirable feature would be to have the area afford a secondary means of escape.

This could be an opening from which to reach the ground safely (not from a high upper floor) or to reach an unobservable intermediate location in the building such as a rear stairwell. (Secondary escape routes from areas with grilled windows/openings would, of course have to be in accordance with fire and safety regulations.)

Even if all elements of a safe haven cannot be achieved, a strong secure area in which to take refuge for a brief period may still be attainable. Of course, in an apartment without accessible openings/windows or balconies, the "safe haven" may be the whole residence, starting with the entrance door.

Long-Term Lease Availability

A factor to consider in the selection of a residence is the availability of a long-term lease. Obtaining such a lease may be particularly desirable if sizeable expenditures are required on security hardware and security-related modifications, as well as on other residence-related expenditures.

Chapter VI. After Moving In

Passport Registration

Take your passport to the U.S. Embassy or Consulate and register as soon as possible following arrival in a foreign country.

All countries abroad where Americans are permitted to conduct business have a U.S. Embassy or American Interests Sector of a friendly embassy in the capital city of that country. In other major population centers there is often times a U.S. Consulate.

Registration greatly facilitates emergency evacuation from the country of residence, if it becomes necessary.

Neighborhood Familiarization

When you have finally moved into your new residence, make an immediate effort to familiarize yourself with your new surroundings. Walk around the neighborhood and drive around the area to get a good idea of where you are located. Note the layout of the streets. Make a mental note of one-way streets. Drive around at night. Streets and buildings look much different in the dark with artificial light.

Get acquainted with at least one neighbor as quickly as possible. You may need a neighbor in an emergency or for a temporary "safe haven" in the event of a burglary or other type of incident.

Learn the location of the nearest hospital and police station. Drive the route to the hospital in daylight and at night. Go directly to the Emergency Room entrance so no time is lost if you really have to use the facility. Check on traffic conditions during rush hours and at other times. Determine how long it will take you to reach the Emergency Room at various times during day and at night.

U.S. Government Advice on Security Concerns

American Embassies and Consulates will upon request, advise any American citizen or business representative on possible terrorist threats in foreign countries. The Regional Security Officer (RSO) or Post Security Officer (PSO) is the point of contact in embassies or consulates who can provide advice and guidance relative to your security concerns. However, it must be noted that the RSO/PSO must limit his assistance to the private sector to security services of an advisory nature. The RSO or other designated officer at a diplomatic or consular post can provide the following information:

- The nature, if any, of the general terrorist threat in a particular country.

- Whether private American citizens or companies have been the target of terrorist threats or attacks in the recent past.

- Specific areas in cities or countryside that are considered dangerous for foreigners.

- Recommended host government contacts, including police officials; local employment requirements for private security services.

- Methods and agencies available for security and background checks on local employees.

- Local laws and regulations concerning ownership, possession, and registration of weapons.

- Local government laws, regulations, and policies on paying ransom or making concessions to terrorists.

U. S. Government Assistance to Terrorist Victims

In the case of a terrorist action against an American citizen or company, the Embassy or Consulate can:

- Facilitate communication with the home office and the family of the victim if normal channels are not adequate.

- Help establish useful liaison with local authorities.

- Provide information and suggest possible alternatives open to the family or company of the victim. The U.S. Government, however, cannot decide whether or not to accede to terrorist demands. Only the family or company of the victim can make such a decision, but it should be in consonance with local law. The official U.S. Government policy, as publicly stated, is not to make any concessions to terrorist demands and, while such policy is not necessarily binding on the private sector, the private sector is well advised to review its proposed action in time of crisis with the Embassy or Consulate.

Unlike some U.S. Government employees who enjoy diplomatic immunity while living and working in the host country, U.S. private sector employees and their families are subject to all laws of the host country. It is well to remember that the constitutional safeguards enjoyed by all Americans in the U.S. do not apply to the actions of foreign governments.)

Emergency Preparations

Once an emergency strikes it is too late to obtain needed equipment or to make necessary preparations, including the following:

- Obtain emergency fire and safety equipment as soon as possible, including but not limited to fire extinguishers, first-aid kits, blankets, matches and candles, flashlights and battery-operated radios with spare batteries. Consider storing a seven-day supply of canned food, juices, water and staples for all members of the family. Supplies should be stored for emergency use and inspected on a regular basis.

- Family members and domestic employees should be trained and tested on the use of each item of emergency equipment.

- Know beforehand where you will turn for help. Familiarize yourself with the identities of nearby neighbors, their servants, and their vehicles. This will facilitate the identification of a stranger or an unauthorized individual in the area.

- Investigate the possibility of participating in an alert-calling list in event of emergencies. If such a list does not exist, create one.

- Be cognizant of host country fire regulations and telephone numbers. Determine if the emergency number has someone on the other end who can understand you if you do not speak the local language. Arrange alternate emergency numbers which can forward your call in the local language if necessary.

- It is highly recommended that an "Employee and Family Profile" form be filled out for each family and updated at least once a year. Keep one copy at home and one at the office with supervisor or person responsible for security. Include current photos of each family member.

Chapter VII. Perimeter Security

General Parameters

Generally, there are two lines of defense for a residence, the outer and the inner perimeter. The outer ordinarily is a property line in the case of a single residence, or the outer lobby door in an apartment or high-rise condominium. A third, or remote outer perimeter, may exist if your home or apartment is situated in a private compound or club environment.

Outer Perimeter

Any perimeter barrier, even if it is only a symbolic hedge, serves as a deterrent. An intruder must commit an overt act in crossing the barrier and run the risk of being seen. Therefore, it is recommended that, where possible, a single-family dwelling overseas have a perimeter barrier.

The type of barrier employed should be carefully considered as each has its advantages and disadvantages. Different type barriers include:

Hedges and Natural Growth Material

This type of barrier is useful in marking the property line. However, unless they are thick and covered with thorns or pointed leaves, they can easily be breached.

Picket and Chain Link Fences

Advantages include view of outside area by resident, while not providing a hiding place for a potential intruder. Residual benefit is restraint for watchdog.

Solid or Block Fences/Walls

Although a solid wall limits the occupant's observation out of the compound and could provide concealment for an intruder, it is usually the most secure perimeter barrier.

The perimeter barrier is no stronger than the gate. A solid wooden gate is appropriate for a hedge or picket fence, a chain link gate is appropriate for a hedge, a picket fence or a chain link fence, and a solid wooden or metal gate is appropriate for a solid fence or wall. The gate should be well anchored to the fence or wall, swing outward with hinges on the inside, and be provided with a high security lock. Keys to locks should be stored in a secure but accessible location in the residence.

Shrubbery around a single detached dwelling should be trimmed in such a way that it does not provide a hiding place.

Consider installation of a contingency or emergency exit through the rear of the property, to be utilized only in high-risk situations.

Inner Perimeter - Grills and Shatter Resistant Film

All building exterior openings over 96 square inches in size on the ground floor or accessible from trees, vehicle tops or porches should be grilled. Bars of solid steel, flat or round stock, spaced five to seven inches apart, with horizontal braces 10-12 inches apart to provide adequate rigidity, and securely imbedded on all sides to a depth of at least three inches into the adjacent wall or frame, should be installed. Use clip anchors or bend the end of the bars when grouting them into the wall. Otherwise, where possible, the bars should extend through the wall and be secured on the interior.

Shatter resistant film, a high-quality clear plastic sheeting glued to windows, is recommended and should be applied to windows and doors before the grills are installed. Decorative grills should be so designed that the protection afforded is equal to the conventional type grills. Wherever possible, grillwork should be installed on the interior of the opening.

At least one grill in each section of the sleeping quarters should be hinged and equipped with an emergency release to permit emergency exit in the event of fire. Houses with a single corridor access to all sleeping quarters should have an iron grill gate to control the bedrooms at nighttime. This grill gate would constitute an inner perimeter protection for the sleeping quarters. Where grillwork is required, a complete early warning fire detection and alarm system must be installed.

Inner Perimeter - Locks and Key Control Locks

These are described in several ways and the various descriptions tend to confuse the layman. For example, they are described by their use (primary or auxiliary), by their locking mechanism (pin tumbler, wafer disc, lever, magnetic, cipher, etc.), by the type of cylinder (single or double), or by the type of mounting (key-in-the-knob, mortised, rim, etc.).

All primary residential entry doors should be equipped with both a primary and auxiliary lock. Additionally, each entry door should have a 190-degree optical viewer or equivalent.

Primary locks are the main lock on a door and are identified by the fact they have handles. These locks are usually key-in-the-knob or mortised type locks with the locking hardware located in a cavity in the door. Unless they have a latch or bolt that extends into the doorjamb 5/8 inch to one inch, they do not provide sufficient protection.

Auxiliary locks usually are deadbolts which are mortise or rim/surface mounted, located on the inner door and doorframe surface, and do not have handles. This type lock does not have to be keyed and may be nothing more than a sliding deadbolt. The exception to this rule is where there is a window or side light within 40 inches of the lock.

Change all exterior locks, including garage door and mailbox lock (if in an apartment) prior to moving into new residence abroad, in either a new or used home. It is possible to change only the lock cylinder or to re-pin the cylinder on good quality locks without changing the complete locking device.

Exterior doors with or near glass panels should be equipped with dead bolts, which are key operated on both interior and exterior. It is advisable to place an extra key for these type locks in a concealed area in the immediate proximity to the inside lock in case of emergencies. All residents should be aware of its location. Never leave the key in the inside lock for personal convenience.

Lock all fuse boxes and electrical panels located on the exterior of the residence.

Electronic garage door openers have advantages and disadvantages and, therefore, should be installed with discretion. A security advantage, in addition to the convenience, is that it is not necessary to leave the security of your locked car to enter and lock your garage behind you. The disadvantage is that such devices can often be compromised by a variety of inexpensive transmitters. If installed, ensure maximum protection is installed on door between garage and interior of house. Discuss with competent locksmith.

Have a qualified locksmith install effective locking devices on sliding glass doors which are highly vulnerable. Avoid using louvered or jalousie windows which are a very easy mark for even the most inexperienced burglar.

Maintaining Perimeter Security

Maintain strict key control on all exterior locks. Never hide an exterior door key outside the house. Sophisticated burglars know all the hiding places.

Install an intercom between primary entrance and the inside foyer or protected area. In apartments and homes the intercom should be backed up with a peep hole in solid core door with an angle of visibility of 190 degrees.

Remove all name identification from your gate and doors. Avoid displays which identify you as an American.

Burglars/terrorists are always on the alert for an easy way to enter a residence. Doors, windows, and garages should be closed and locked at all times when the residents are away from home, no matter how short the time. If there is any doubt about accountability of keys to a home, have the lock cylinders replaced or re-pinned. Keys should be controlled and only given to mature family members or trusted friends. When domestic employees are given a key, it should only be to the primary lock of one entry door. They should never be given keys to both the primary and auxiliary locks. This ensures that the occupants can always secure the residence in the evenings or when the domestic staff is absent.

Ensure that access to the residence is not permitted through domestic employee's quarters.

Any padlocks used for residential security should always be stored in the locked position. Sophisticated burglars sometimes will replace a padlock with a similar one to which they alone have the key.

Chapter VIII. Intrusion Alarms and Security Lighting

Objective

Intrusion or alerting devices are any means by which a resident and/or the local police/security force are made aware of the attempted or forcible entry of a residence. This includes alarm systems, guards, dogs, noisemakers, and communications systems.

Alarm Systems

Basically, alarm systems perform two functions: they detect an intruder, and they report the intrusion. However, for the purpose of residential security use overseas, an alarm system in a residence should be considered as a deterrent device. In areas abroad where forced entry of a residence is commonplace, or where an active terrorist threat is present, the use of a good residential alarm system is highly recommended.

Minimum desired alarm system features are:

- Capable of operating on the local electrical current and have a rechargeable battery backup.

- Relatively easy to install and trouble-shoot. Many local electricians may not be capable of installing or repairing a complex alarm system.

- Equipped with a time delay feature to allow the occupant to arm or disarm the system without activating the alarm.

- Capable of being wired with a fixed or mobile panic switch, a device which permits manual activation of the alarm system. Panic switches should be installed in the safe haven, in the living portion of the residence and outside as well for use by residential guards.

Security Lighting

Security lighting should be an integral part of the intrusion system.

Lighting - Most intruders will go to great lengths to escape visual detection. Therefore, they will normally strike at a residence that appears vacant or is dark.

Outdoor lighting can be a major deterrent against criminal intrusion. Properly used, it can discourage criminal activity and aid observation.

The important elements of protective outdoor lighting are coverage and evenness of light. It is possible that in some residential settings existing street lighting, along with one or two porch lights, will furnish sufficient lighting. However, it may be necessary to install additional lighting in order to achieve the degree of security desired. If outdoor lighting is to be used as a protective measure, all accesses to vulnerable areas of the property and house should be lighted.

Lighting should be placed in such a manner that it covers the walls of the residence and the ground area adjacent to the perimeter walls. Also, it should illuminate shrubbery and eliminate building blind spots.

If security lighting is deemed advisable in your location, it should consist of two independent systems. Cosmetic or low-level tamper-resistant fixtures installed in the eaves or overhangs for continuous perimeter illumination, and emergency floodlights tied to the alarm system so that they will turn on automatically when the alarm is activated. A manual switch should be installed in the living quarters of the single-family residence, so that they may be turned on independent of the alarm system.

It is a good idea to connect the cosmetic lighting to a photo electric cell which automatically turns them on at dusk and off at dawn. They should be connected to a dimmer, so that the light level can be adjusted to the extent that it would discourage an attack on the house by burglars but at the same time would not be offensive to the neighbors.

Ensure that all lighting systems are installed in compliance with local codes.

Consider installation of diesel-powered auxiliary generator which turns on automatically when electric power fails. Turn on at least once each quarter to insure it's in good working order.

"Mushroom" lights which are installed along the foundation of the house and cast a light up the side of the structure are easily compromised and should be avoided.

Chapter IX. Extended Absences From the Residence

Extended absences present the burglar with his easiest opportunity to target a residence. There are many indicators to a burglar that a residence is unoccupied. For example, discussing the planned absence in the office or in the neighborhood, forgetting to cancel deliveries, leaving the home unlighted and the blinds or drapes drawn, and closing the shutters.

While residents are away, automatic timers or photoelectric switches should turn on inside lights, a radio, or even an air-conditioner to create the illusion that someone is home.

Invite a reliable neighbor to park a car in your driveway at times during your absence, especially at night.

Ask close friends or neighbors to look after the home and turn on and off different lights, put out trash as usual, etc.

In many foreign locations it is advisable to have trusted domestic employees remain in the residence during extended absences.

If you live in a single-family house or if the servants are on vacation, you could hire a guard but do not give him access to enter the house. He should only patrol the garden area which encircles the house.

Hook up of a telephone answering device serves to defeat the telephone call that is made by the terrorist/criminal to determine if someone is home.

Chapter X. Domestic Hires Screening and Responsibilities

Domestic employees can either be a valuable asset to residential security or a decided liability. The chances of obtaining the services of a reliable servant can be improved by hiring one employed and recommended by a friend, acquaintance or neighbor.

Prospective applicants should be required to produce references and should be interviewed thoroughly.

It is wise to personally check with references to confirm their existence and obtain information concerning the reliability, honesty, attitudes and work habits of prospective applicants.

In some countries, the authorities will conduct background investigations upon request.

In some foreign countries, it is an accepted practice to request full personal data from applicants for employment. This data should be copied from either a National Government I.D. card or a passport.

Do not accept the person's word as to their name and date of birth without an authentic government document to back up their claim.

Obtain the following information:

- Government Identity Card or passport, etc., for number, date of birth, nationality, full names, valid date, place of registry.

- Letters of reference: Be sure you know who wrote it and what it says. (Usually written in local language.)

- Obtain the address of the former employer and the company he represented.

- Good domestic employees are generally referred by your predecessor, although this is not always the case.

This entire procedure should only require a few days if you utilize good contacts with competent police recommended by the embassy, consulate or your predecessor. If you are unable to establish good contacts, contract the job out to reliable investigative consultants.

Caution

Do not permit domestics of untested integrity and reliability in your home. If you must engage a cook or house servant before investigation is completed, do not entrust keys or an unoccupied house to the employee in question.

When you have hired a servant, record his/her complete name, date and place of birth, identity card number, telephone number, and address as well as the names of spouse, parent or close relative.

Domestic help should be briefed on security practices. It is critical that they be rehearsed and re-briefed from time to time to refresh their memory and to update previous instructions. Domestic staff should be briefed on visitor control, how to report suspicious or unusual activity, proper telephone answering procedures, and admittance of maintenance men to the residence. They should also be made aware of emergency telephone numbers. They should be able to reach the man or woman of the house by phone to report critical situations at the residence.

Domestic employees should be trained to answer the door rather than members of the household. They should not be allowed to admit visitors without specific approval. When visitors, repair or services personnel are expected, domestic employees should be informed of their probable time of arrival and identification and should not unlock or open the door until they have been properly identified.

Domestic employees should never give a caller the impression that no one is home, nor should they tell when the occupants are expected. They should be directed to reply that occupants are "Unable to come to the phone right now but will return the call, if the caller will leave his name and telephone number."

Domestic employees should not be allowed to overhear family plans and official business. Sensitive and confidential letters such as those dealing with business strategies, hiring or firing practices, employee disciplinary matters and other matters which are closely guarded at the office, should be equally guarded at home. Travel itineraries, purchasing negotiations and bids, labor negotiation strategies, pricing and marketing information, to name but a few, are other examples of official business which should not be shared with domestics in any form, written or oral, and documents relating to same should not be left unsecured about the residence.

Terrorists or burglars do not always break in; sometimes people let them in. Family members should be wary of salesmen, or unexpected visits from repairmen or utility company representatives, even if they are in uniform. Ask to see their credentials or call their office to verify their bona fides. If a stranger asks to use the telephone, do not let him in. Make the call for him. Do not hesitate to be suspicious if the situation warrants it. An intercom system can be used to determine a stranger's business before he is allowed access to the residence.

Frequently brief all domestic hires, such as maids, cooks, gardeners, handymen and chauffeurs, on security precautions. Be very specific in making clear what you expect of them. It is advisable to select one member of the domestic staff and make him/her responsible for the actions of others.

Instruct the domestic help to report to the man or woman of the house the presence of strangers in the neighborhood. Virtually all kidnappings and terrorist assaults have indicated that the perpetrators had an intimate knowledge of the victims' habits developed through surveillance prior to attack.

Do not allow domestic help to invite anyone into your home without prior approval.

As a final word of caution, do not, in front of domestic employees, make comments which could be construed as being disrespectful of local customs or people. Even when they make critical remarks about themselves or their government do not join in. Remember that we would probably consider criticism of the U.S. by a foreigner even if justified as an indication of anti-Americanism, especially if made repeatedly. And remember further, the security of you and your family may depend on these employees and their fellow nationals.

Chapter XI. Family and Company Cars

Selection of Make and Model

Purchase or lease a car that blends in well with local passenger car environment. Remember to keep a low profile!

Safety and Security Precautions:

- Consider installation of burglar alarm on car consistent with risk level.

- Make sure gas cap, spare tire, and engine compartment are lockable in the interest of good safety and security.

- Always have the fuel tank at least half full.

- Keep vehicle(s) locked at all times.

- Never park your vehicle on the street for long periods of time.

- Keep your vehicle(s) housed in a garage.

- Make sure that you have both right and left side rear view mirrors.

- Visibility around your vehicle is critical.

- Do not leave registration papers in your car.

- If legal to do so, have your car license plate registered to a Post Office Box rather than to your home or office. List the P.O. Box to your office.

- Keep extra water and oil in the trunk.

- Keep emergency equipment in the trunk - flashlight, flares, fire extinguisher, first aid kit, etc.

- Do not use stickers or personalized license plates.

- If possible, install a communication device, such as a two-way radio or telephone in your car.

Chapter XII. Auto Travel

Travel Precautions

Potential victims of kidnapping and assault are probably most vulnerable when entering or leaving their home or office.

- Never enter a car without checking the rear seat to ensure that it is empty.

- Do not develop predictable patterns during the business day or during free time. For example, do not leave home or the office at the same time and by the same route every day. Do not have a standard tee-off time for golf, tennis, hand ball, etc.

- If possible, exchange company cars, swap with co-workers occasionally.

- Know the location of police, hospital, military, and government buildings. Ascertain when they are open and which are 24-hour operations. These areas can provide a safe haven along normal transportation routes.

- Even the slightest disruption in travel patterns may disrupt a surveillance team sufficiently for them to tip their hand or abandon their efforts.

- Avoid trips to remote areas, particularly after dark. If it is essential to go into such an area, travel in a group or convoy and advise trusted personnel of your itinerary.

- Select well-traveled streets as much as possible.

- Keep vehicles well maintained at all times, including a useable spare tire. Install additional rear-view mirrors so passengers may see what is behind.

- If chauffeur driven, consider riding up front next to the driver sometimes, in keeping with the low-profile concept.

- Chauffeurs and high-risk personnel should be trained in offensive and evasive driving techniques.

- When driving, keep doors and windows locked.

- Be constantly alert to road conditions and surroundings, to include possible surveillance by car, motorcycle, or bicycle. All passengers should be vigilant. If surveillance or some other danger is detected, drive to the closest safe haven, such as police station, hospital emergency room, fire station, etc., lock your car and go inside. Advise authorities as appropriate.

- When traveling, pre-plan your route and one alternate.

- Be prepared for local environmental conditions (snow, rain, etc.).

- Never pick up hitchhikers.

- Whenever possible, drive to the center of the road, especially in rural settings, to avoid being forced off the road.

- Remain a safe distance behind the vehicle ahead to allow space for avoidance maneuvers, if necessary.

- Check side and rear-view mirrors routinely.

- Carry 3 x 5 cards with important assistance phrases printed on them to assist with language problems. Always carry appropriate coin denomination for public phones. Practice use of public telephones.

- Report as appropriate all suspicious activity to the company security contact, embassy or consulate, or local police as soon as possible.

- Consider keeping a small hand-held cassette recorder in the glove box at all times, descriptions of suspicious persons, activities, license plate numbers, etc., can be dictated while driving. It's impossible to make notes while driving or in stressful situations.

- Never leave identifying material or valuables in the vehicle.

Surveillance

If surveillance is suspected, consider the following actions:

- Divert from originally intended destination, make a few turns to see if the surveillant still persists.

- Immediately determine any identifying data that you can observe. (For example: make, color of car, license number, number and description of occupants.)

- Remember; do not panic if surveillance is confirmed. Surveillance teams are normally neither trained nor have the mission to assault the potential target.

Parking Precautions

- Always lock the vehicle, no matter where it is located.\

- Do not leave the car in the care of a valet parking service such as hotel, restaurant or club.

- Require chauffeurs to stay with the car.

- Avoid leaving the vehicle parked on the street overnight.

- Never exit vehicle without checking the area for suspicious individuals. If in doubt, drive away.

Chapter XIII. Telephones

One can never be sure of the true identity of a person on the other end of a telephone line. For this reason, it behooves all of us to exercise the following telephone security precautions:

- Do not answer the telephone by stating the name of the family.

- If a caller inquires, "To whom am I speaking?", respond with a question like, "Who are you calling?"

- Do not give the residence telephone number in response to wrong-number telephone calls. If the caller asks, "What number did I reach?" respond with another question like, "What number are you calling?"

- Report repetitive wrong-number telephone calls to the telephone company, the person in charge of security at your company, if there is such a person, and to the police as appropriate.

- Be suspicious of any caller alleging to represent the telephone company and advising that the telephone service may be interrupted.

- Be skeptical of telephone calls from strangers advising that a family member has been injured or has won a prize, or making any other assertion that is followed by a request for the family member to leave the home immediately. Verify the telephone call by looking up the number of the caller in the directory, check it against the one given by the caller, and then call the number to verify the information given.

- Children should be advised not to converse with strangers on the telephone for any reason. When an adult is not present, a child will occasionally answer the phone. Children should be instructed to tell callers in such circumstances that the adult being called is not available to come to the phone, rather than reveal that the adult is absent from the home.

- When practical, home telephone numbers should be unlisted and unpublished.

- Do not list home phone numbers in company directories unless circulation is highly restricted.

- Family members and domestic help should not divulge personal information or travel plans over the telephone to anyone without specific authority to do so.

- Avoid party lines.

- Consider use of answering devices for ALL incoming calls in order to be selective in which calls you choose to answer.

- Report ALL suspicious activity to your security contact at the company or the local police.

- Locate the nearest public telephone to your home and inform the family and household members of its location for their use in an emergency. Also, locate the nearest non-public telephone to your home to which you have access, perhaps a friendly neighbor's phone, for the same reason.

- All family members should carry the phone number of one or more trusted neighbors who have a clear view of your home, either front or rear. A pseudo-extortionist may call you at your office and claim that family member(s) are being held at gunpoint at your home and, unless a sum of money is paid to a third party or placed at a designated location, they will be harmed. A telephone call to a neighbor who has a clear view of your home may, by simply looking out the window, determine that your family is in no jeopardy at all and thereby determine with reasonable certainty that the call is a hoax. If a strange vehicle is parked in the driveway, the police should be notified as appropriate.

- Emergency telephone numbers of police, fire, medical and ambulance service should be available for quick reference at each telephone in the home. Check accuracy of list every six months or so.

- You and your family members should practice the use of public telephones.

- If available, maintain two portable two-way radios - one in your own home and one in a neighbor's home - in the event wire communications are severed. Telephone service in many foreign countries is highly unreliable.

- In certain emergencies, it may become necessary on short notice to locate and account for all members of the family. Make it a habit to know generally where family members will be every day. Make a list of phone numbers of all places frequently visited by family members such as neighbors, friends' homes, clubs, beauty salons, barbers, favorite restaurants, schools, etc. All family members should carry a copy of the list and a copy kept at home for domestics and one at the office. Update regularly.

Chapter XIV. Mail

Businessmen should discourage the delivery of mail to their private residence. Either rent a Post Office Box registered to your office or have your personal mail delivered to your office.

Family members and domestic help should accept no mail parcels or other unexpected deliveries unless they are sure of the source.

Do not open the door to accept strange deliveries. Packages should be left near the door. Wait a considerable time before opening the door to retrieve the package.

If deliveryman requires a signature, have him slide receipt under the door.

Continuously remind yourself and others in the household to be suspicious of all incoming mail and parcels and to remain alert for the following danger signs:

Appearance

- Is it from a strange place?

- Is there an excessive amount of postage?

- Are there stains on the item?

- Are wires or strings protruding or attached to the item in an unusual location?

- Is the item marked conspicuously with the receiver's name: i.e., Personal for Mr. Smith, Confidential for Mr. Smith?

- Is the spelling on the item correct?

- Does the letter or package contain an inner letter or package addressed to a particular individual or tied with a string, tape, wire, rubber band, or any compression item?

- Do the return address and the postmark differ?

Odor

- Do the items smell peculiar? Many explosives used by terrorists smell like shoe polish or almonds.

Weight

- Is the item unusually heavy or light?

- Is the item uneven in balance or lopsided?

Caution

If parcel is at all suspicious, STOP further handling, place item against exterior corner of room. DO NOT IMMERSE ITEM IN WATER. This may make paper soggy and cause spring-loaded device to detonate. Open windows and evacuate the immediate area. Call appropriate authorities.

Chapter XV. Banking and Charge Accounts

Checking accounts, charge accounts and loan applications create audit trails which divulge more about you and your family than you may wish to be known. Purchasing habits can reveal much about the value of household goods and personal valuables that are kept in your residence and which might become attractive to potential thieves. It may be prudent to utilize major U.S. credit cards as opposed to writing checks on local banks, in order to reduce the audit trail your financial transactions can leave.

When requested to write a phone number on checks or credit card slips, use the office number and have family members do the same.

DO NOT imprint your home address or phone number on personalized checks.

Chapter XVI. Trash Removal

Trash containers have been proven to be excellent sources of intelligence for curiosity seekers and terrorists. Therefore, do not place material in them which can be exploited to the detriment of yourself or a member of your family. To preclude this possibility, incinerate, disintegrate or shred trash consisting of private papers, letters, correspondence including drafts of outgoing correspondence, bills, invoices, cancelled checks as well as any papers with your signature or facsimile thereof, or any other type of materials which might result in embarrassment to or compromise the security of any other member of your household. As a rule of thumb, all paper products, used carbons and discs or tapes, exclusive of wrapping paper and publications not annotated by a member of your household should be destroyed as indicated above.

Trash receptacles should be stored inside the residence or outside in a secure shed, to preclude easy access by the curiosity seeker or the placement of dangerous objects.

Chapter XVII. Quality of Law Enforcement Protection

Police Capability

Assessment of police protection available to a given area is necessary. Determine if the police have sufficient officers and means of transportation and communication to respond to residential crimes in a timely manner. Every effort should be expended to establish quick, dependable communication links to the local security or police force to insure their effective response in an emergency. You should be aware of the attitude of the government, police and the populace towards other nationals, particularly Americans. A strong anti-American attitude may be cause for diminished police responsiveness.

Private Guard Service

Where police capability is in doubt, the use of a private guard service should be considered. However, the use of guards is costly and the quality of guards varies significantly from area to area. Most guards are poorly trained and ineffective. However, if the guard can at least alert the resident to an attack on the residence by tripping a "panic" switch, sounding a horn, or blowing a whistle, he has done his job.

All guards should be subjected to a security check. As much as possible should be known about the employed guards, particularly where and how effectively he has worked previously. At a minimum, guards should be physically capable of performing their shift duties during the normal work day. They should be provided with the following: written guard orders (both in English and native language), a uniform, a communication or alerting device, e.g., air horn, whistle, alarm panic switch, two-way radio, etc., a flashlight, and a defensive weapon such as a club or a chemical deterrent (mace). In rare instances where the threat warrants and local laws and customs allow, a side arm should be considered provided the guard is fully trained in its use.

Chapter XVIII. Firearms in Foreign Countries

Firearms restrictions and/or requirements differ from country to country. Persons assigned overseas should contact the local police authority to ascertain the law of the land concerning private ownership of weapons.

If authorized by the host country, weapons must be maintained and used in accordance with the local customs and laws. Host country licenses must be obtained when required. Training and safety should be prime considerations if a weapon is to be maintained in the home.

Illegal importation of a firearm is a serious criminal offense in many countries.

Chapter XIX. Children's School

When children are to be picked up at school by other than immediate family members, there should be an established procedure coordinated with school officials to assure that they are picked up only by authorized persons.

Children should be instructed in observing good security procedures such as traveling in groups, refusing rides with strangers, avoiding isolated play areas, keeping parents informed as to time and destination, reporting all strange events and attempted molestations and how to get help or call the police.

In many overseas locations it is economical to contract with a taxi company or driver to pick up and drop off students at school and home. Insist on the same driver every day and instruct children not to ride with a strange driver. In other locations carpooling may be practical.

Chapter XX. Coups d'etat and Emergency Evacuations

Establish contact, if not done so earlier, and maintain continuing contact with the Regional Security Officer (RSO) or Post Security Officer (PSO) at the nearest U.S. diplomatic post, i.e. Embassy or Consulate, and a designated member(s) of the Emergency Action Committee. Each post abroad formulates an Emergency Action Plan unique to its location, to deal with a coup d'etat and an attempted coup.

- DO NOT automatically pack and leave the country on your own initiative. Most coups only last a few days and are usually preceded by some type of advance warning, such as demonstrations, and therefore, often times can be anticipated. Contact the RSO/PSO for guidance BEFORE taking drastic action.

- Monitor local news media, TV, radio and newspapers for any evidence of anti-American activity, since such activity will have an impact on the Embassy's Emergency Action Plan.

- In certain locations, for example in some third world countries, where the political climate is right for coups and coup attempts, it is recommended that adequate supplies of non-perishable foods and drinking water be stockpiled in your home to sustain your family for an arbitrary period of time (days or weeks) consistent with the existing threat. Maintain regular (at least daily) contact with the Embassy during such periods of high stress.

- Develop alternate routes of evacuation from your residence to be used in the event of fire or other emergency where rapid evacuation would be necessary.

- Be prepared. Have bag packed for each family member in the event you have to leave on short notice.

- Appropriate amount of currency and traveler's checks should be isolated and kept on hand.

- Keep airline tickets (without reservations) on hand for each family member.

- Maintain current passports and, where applicable, visas for a "safe haven" country.

- Prepare a list of telephone numbers for transportation companies, should emergency evacuation be necessary, i.e., taxi, airlines, private limousine service, etc. Place near the office and home telephones.

- Consolidate important personal records/files for easy access and transportation.

- Have more than one (1) evacuation plan.

- Americans should have in place a pre-planned telephonic pyramid contact system, to ensure the American population in the host country is aware of what is happening. A pyramid contact system is one in which each person called with information is required to call two or three others to relay the same information.

Chapter XXI. Social Activities

- During social gatherings, conversations with citizens of host country, especially with reference to political, racial, economic, religious and controversial local issues, should be closely guarded and as non-committal as possible.

- Where possible, employees in high threat areas should avoid social activities which have a set place and schedule, such as the same church service every Sunday morning, shopping at the same store every Saturday, and attending well publicized American citizen functions.

Chapter XXII. Spouse and Dependent Activity

Each family member should be familiar with basic security procedures and techniques.

- All family members should know how to use the local telephones, both public and private.

- Family members should not reveal information concerning travel or other family plans; they should be cautious in answering such questions over the phone, even if the caller is known, to guard against the possibility of taps or other leaks.

- Family members should avoid local civil disturbances, demonstrations, crowds, or other high-risk areas.

- Children, in particular, should be on guard against being approached or questioned by strangers. It is safer to drive them to school than to let them walk. If they must walk, they should not go alone. Adult escorts are preferable, but even groups of children offer some deterrence. Although children must attend school on a particular schedule, parents are encouraged to vary departures, arrivals, and routes to the extent possible. Use of carpools, especially if scheduling is on a random basis, also breaks down patterns of movement and enhances security.

- The location of family members should be known at all times. Causes of delays or unforeseen absences should be determined immediately. Family members should be encouraged to develop the habit of checking in before departure, after arrival, or when changing plans.

- Shopping or family outings should not conform to a set pattern or routine.

Chapter XXIII. Watchdogs

- A dog's extremely sensitive and discriminating senses of smell and hearing enable it to detect quickly a stranger who is not normally present in the residential area. The well-trained dog will normally bark ferociously when approached by an intruder.

- Dogs should be well trained to react only to the introduction of strangers into the residence area, to stop barking on command from the owner, and to accept food only from its master.

- Sophisticated burglars can neutralize the most ferocious of watchdogs by tossing it a meat patty laced with Demerol, which will put the dog to sleep for several hours.

- There are some liabilities attached to the presence of an animal whose role is to deter, discourage, and rout criminal intruders, particularly if the animal does not discriminate well between friend and foe.

Chapter XXIV. Recreation and Exercise

In order to establish a potential target's routine and evaluate the level of security awareness, terrorists usually watch their intended victims for some time before they attack. Therefore, persons in high threat areas should consider whether or not to participate in recreational or exercise activities which have a set place and schedule such as: bowling, little league sports, golf, tennis, jogging, walking, etc.

If you decide to participate in these sports, you should select jogging paths, tennis courts, golf clubs and all out-of-door activity locations with great care. For example, do not indiscriminately jog through a park with which you are not totally familiar. Use densely populated areas, if possible.

Chapter XXV. A Word About Illegal Drugs

Despite repeated warnings, drug arrests and convictions of American citizens are still on the increase. If you are caught with either soft or hard drugs overseas, you are subject to local and not U.S. laws. Penalties for possession or trafficking are often the same.

The laws governing the use, possession, and trafficking in illegal drugs vary widely throughout the world, as do penalties for violations of those laws. One may be legal in one country and may constitute a serious criminal offense in another. It behooves all U.S. Citizens living abroad to familiarize themselves with selected laws of the host country, especially those relating to illegal drugs.

A statement by Mr. John C. Lawn, while he was Administrator of the Drug Enforcement Administration, U.S. Department of Justice, emphasized the seriousness of violations of illegal drug laws abroad and resultant penalties:

"Possession and use of illegal drugs overseas is no casual matter. Unlike the United States, in many countries trafficking and even possessing drugs for personal use are extremely serious offenses. You may have no rights at all - no bail, no speedy trial, no jury trial - the penalties can be severe and the prisons can be frightening. You are subject to the criminal sanctions of another country. In at least two countries I know of, the penalty includes death and the U.S. State Department will not be able to help you."

It is important that the foregoing be emphasized to all family members living abroad, especially to teenage children and young adults.

Prescription Medications

It is advisable to leave all medicines in their original labeled containers if you require medication containing habit-forming drugs or narcotics. You should also carry a copy of the doctor's prescription. These precautions will make customs processing easier and also will ensure you do not violate the laws of the country where you plan to live or are currently residing.

Chapter XXVI. A Word About Bomb Threats, Bombings, Extortion and Kidnapping

Bomb threats, bombings, extortion, kidnapping, and hostage taking are criminal acts frequently engaged in by international terrorists. We have alluded to these techniques in this booklet in only a general way. It was not the intention of the authors to expound on these highly volatile subjects in detail, since so much has already been written about them.

Chapter XXVII. Conclusion

Many of us have been victimized by crime and most of us are acquainted with victims of crime. The news media daily swamps us with a barrage of stories about a wide range of criminal activities, including burglary, robbery, rape, kidnapping and murder, to name but a few. To this list have been added, in recent years, the often bizarre activities of the international political terrorist, which are nonetheless criminal acts. Yet, it is perhaps the most difficult job in the world to convince people to practice security and safety in their lives.

Crime is escalating throughout the world. It is a most serious problem, which will not be solved in our lifetime, if ever. Unfortunately, we cannot delegate our personal security to the police or to anyone else. Law enforcement, as we all know, is largely reactive.

Each of us must assume responsibility for our personal security and insure that our loved ones do the same. We must adopt an attitude of continuous awareness to our vulnerabilities and always resist the temptation to yield to the complacent philosophy of "it will not happen to me."

If we do not involve ourselves, personally, in protecting our loved ones, our property, and ourselves our vulnerability to criminal acts will increase dramatically.

Security, like safety, will never be a positive science because there are no foolproof techniques or hardware, which guarantee freedom from vulnerability. Effective security must be dynamic and never static simply because the diverse risks which confront us are always changing.

Remember always to remain vigilant, especially in the unfamiliar environment of faraway places.

RESIDENTIAL SECURITY SURVEY

NEIGHBORHOOD

1. Is unit in good residential area with a low crime rate?

2. Do other employees live nearby?

3. Is the police and fire protection adequate and within 10-minute response time?

4. Are there a number of alternate routes to and from the dwelling?

EXTERIOR OF SINGLE-FAMILY OR DUPLEX DWELLING

1. Is the property well defined with a hedge, fence or wall in good condition?

2. Are the gates solid and in good condition?

RESIDENTIAL SECURITY SURVEY

3. Are gates kept locked?

4. Are there handy access routes (poles, trees, etc.), which may be used to get over the barrier?

5. Is public or residence lighting sufficient to illuminate all sides of the dwelling?

6. Are all lights working at sufficient height to prevent tampering?

7. Have hiding places near doors, windows & garage or parking area been illuminated or eliminated?

8. If garage is available, is it used and kept locked?

EXTERIOR OF APARTMENT

1. Are the public areas of the building controlled and well lighted?

2. Can lobby and elevator be viewed from the street?

3. Are secondary entrances to the building and parking controlled?

4. Is apartment height within the rescue capabilities (ladder height) of the fire department?

5. Is the balcony (or other apartment windows) accessible from another balcony, ledge, roof or window?

DOORS

1. Can each exterior (regular, sliding, French, etc.) door be adequately secured?

2. Does the primary lock on each door work?

3. Are all doors kept locked?

4. Can any door be opened from the outside by breaking a door glass or sidelight?

5. Have all unused exterior doors been permanently secured?

6. Are all keys accounted for?

7. Have all "hidden" keys (under door mat, etc.) been removed?

8. Are exterior hinges protected?

9. Does each major entrance have a door viewer or interview grille?

WINDOWS

1. Are all non-ventilating windows permanently secured?

2. Are all windows accessible from the ground, balconies, trees, ledges, roofs and the like protected by grilles?

3. Are all windows kept closed and locked when not in use?

4. Have emergency escape provisions been incorporated into one or more window grilles?

5. Are all sliding and hinged glass doors secured with a metal grille gate?

6. Are all sliding glass doors and windows secured by a rod (charlie bar) in the slide track?

7. Are windows and wall air conditioners anchored and protected by steel grille-work to prevent removal from the outside?

ALARMS

1. Are all entrance doors alarmed?

2. Are all non-grilled windows within access of the ground, balconies, trees, etc. alarmed?

3. Does the alarm have an external alerting device, such as a bell or siren?

4. Is the alarm linked by transmitter to a central monitor station?

5. Does the system have panic buttons placed at strategic locations around the residence?

6. Do the occupants test the alarm periodically?

SAFEHAVEN

1. If a safe haven is recommended, can one be accommodated?

2. Does the safe haven have a solid core, metal, or metal-clad door?

3. Is the emergency radio kept charged and available in the safe haven?

4. Are toilet facilities available in the safe haven?

5. Is there an emergency egress from the safe haven?

MISCELLANEOUS CONCERNS

1. Does the dwelling have at least one 5 lb. or 10 lb. ABC general-purpose fire extinguisher located in the kitchen?

2. Does the dwelling have at least one 2 1/2 gallon water type fire extinguisher located in the safe haven?

3. Are fire extinguishers checked periodically?

4. Do the occupants, including older children & domestic employees, know how to use extinguishers?

5. Is there a smoke detector in the dwelling?

6. Are smoke detectors properly installed?

7. Are smoke detector batteries replaced at least once a year?

8. Are smoke detectors tested periodically?

9. Does the dwelling have an operational emergency radio, with an outside antenna?

10. Do the occupants, including older children and domestic employees, know how to use the radio?

11. Are emergency phone numbers (post, fire, police, ambulance) kept near the phone?

12. Has a background check been conducted on domestic employees?

13. Have children and employees been briefed on security requirements (locked windows & doors, no admittance of strangers, no acceptance of packages, etc.)?

14. Do occupants have a firearm in the home?

15. Is it protected (trigger lock, disassembled, etc.) from children?

16. Have occupants been trained in its use?

EXTERIOR

1. Do garden gates lock?

2. Are gates kept locked and the keys under your control?

3. Is the gate bell in working order?

4. Are stairways lighted?

5. Are walls of sufficient height to deter thieves?

6. Are exterior lights adequate to illuminate the residence grounds, particularly around gates and doors?

7. If butane gas is used, are the bottles secured in a safe place?

8. Are there any poles, boxes, trees, or outbuildings that would help an intruder scale your wall or fence?

BUILDING DOORS

1. Are the exterior doors of solid wood or metal construction?

2. Are locks on your exterior doors of the cylinder type?

3. Are they the dead locking (jimmy-proof) type?

4. Can any of your door locks be opened by breaking a glass or light wood panel next to the lock?

5. Do you use heavy-duty sliding deadbolts on your most used doors as auxiliary locks?

6. Can all your doors including porch, balcony, basement, terrace and roof be locked securely?

7. Are all your locks in good working order?

8. Does anyone other than your immediate family have a key to your residence (i.e., previous tenants, owners, servants, friends)?

9. Are all unused doors permanently secured?

10. Are all locks securely mounted?

11. Do you hide a spare key to your main entrance under a door mat, in a flower pot, or some other nearby, but obvious, spot?

12. Do you answer the door partially dressed?

13. Do you have a peephole or interview grille in your main door?

14. Do you answer the door without first checking to see who has rung the bell or knocked?

15. Do you lock your padlocks in place when the doors are unlocked (garage, storage room, unused servants' quarters, etc.)?

16. Are padlock hasps installed so that screws cannot be removed?

17. Are hasps and staple plates mounted so that they cannot be pried or twisted off?

WINDOWS

1. Are all your first-floor windows protected?

2. Are unused windows permanently closed and sealed?

3. Are your windows properly and securely mounted?

4. Can window locks be opened by breading the glass?

5. Do you keep your windows locked when they are shut?

6. Are you as careful with securing windows on the second floor or basement windows as you are with those on the ground floor?

7. Have you locked up your ladder or relocated trellises that might be used as a ladder to gain entry through a second-story window?

8. Do you have a sliding glass door and if so, do you have a rod or "charlie bar" to place in the track?

GARAGE

1. Do you lock your garage at night and when you are away from home?

2. Are all garage doors and windows equipped with adequate locks and are they in good working order?

3. Are tools and equipment left in the garage where a burglar might be able to use them in gaining entry to your residence?

MISCELLANEOUS

1. Do you have any type of fire extinguishers?

2. Do you know the type of fire on which to use your extinguishers?

3. Has your firefighting equipment been inspected or recharged within the past year?

4. Does every member of your family and domestic staff know how to use your firefighting equipment?

5. Do you keep your cash and small valuables in a safe storage place?

6. Do you have a list of serial numbers of your watches, cameras, typewriters, computers, radios, stereo, VTRs, etc.?

7. Do you keep an inventory of all valuable property?

8. Do you have an accurate description (with photographs) of all valuable property which does not have serial numbers?

9. Do you avoid unnecessary display or publicity of your valuable items?

10. Have you given your family and servants instructions on what they should do if they discover an intruder attempting to break in or already in the house?

11. Have you told your family and servants to leave the house undisturbed and call the police if they find a burglary has been committed?

12. Do you know and have you posted near the telephone the number of the nearest police station?

13. Do you know how to report a fire and your dwelling location in the local language?

14. Do you and your family have an emergency escape plan with alternate emergency escape routes? Have you practiced this emergency plan?

15. Have you instructed your family and servants regarding the admission of strangers, no

matter how authentic their credentials may appear?

16. Are you, your family, and servants alert in the observations of strange vehicles or persons who may have you under surveillance or may be "casing" your residence for a burglary?

17. Have you verified the references and good health of your servants?

18. Do you know the location and telephone number of the nearest police, fire department, and hospital?

Security Guidelines for American Enterprises Abroad

Effective security precautions require a continuous and conscious awareness of your environment. This is especially true when living in a foreign country where it will be necessary to adapt to new cultures, customs, and laws, which, in most instances, are very different from those to which Americans are accustomed in the United States.

The implementation of security guidelines contained in this publication could reduce the vulnerability of American private sector enterprises abroad to criminal or terrorist acts. It is recognized that some of the recommended guidelines cannot easily be implemented at existing facilities.

Chapter I. Introduction

This booklet is a compilation of security guidelines for American private sector executives operating outside the United States. This guidance is the product of many years of experience by a cross section of American security practitioners from both the public and private sectors. Obviously, the implementation should be consistent with the level of risk in the country where you conduct business. For the most part the guidelines are for protection in high threat areas. It is recognized that the level of risk varies from country to country and time to time so that you may need to choose among the suggested options or apply the concepts in a manner modified to meet your needs. Since levels of risk can change very rapidly, it is advisable to continuously monitor factors that may impact the risk level. Security precautions must be flexible and dynamic to respond effectively to changing risks. A static, inflexible security posture will almost certainly result in a lack of preparedness or unnecessary expense.

The Department of State has three threat assessment designators: High, Medium, and Low. One of these three threat designators is applied to each country where the United States has diplomatic representation. Threat assessment information is available to the American business community in countries where the United States has diplomatic representation through the Regional Security Officer or Post Security Officer at the nearest U.S. diplomatic post, i.e. Embassy or Consulate. The level assigned to a particular country is determined by an analysis of the political, terrorist, and criminal environment of that country. It is reviewed quarterly by the Department of State and changed when appropriate.

A High Threat country is one where the threat is serious and forced entries and assaults on residents are common, or where an active terrorist threat exists. A Medium Threat country is one where the threat is moderate, with some forced entries and assaults on residents occurring, or where the area has the potential for terrorist activity. A Low Threat country is one where the threat is minimal and forced entry of residences and assault of occupants is not common, and there is no known terrorist threat.

For emphasis again, the guidelines set forth in this publication are generally most appropriate for High Threat areas. One will probably want to moderate them for applications where the risk is lower; or where other considerations preclude their implementation at the level discussed here. In many situations, professional technical security assistance will be required.

These guidelines emphasize site selection and operational security. Appendices I and II are checklists which will help you determine your security needs.

Chapter II. Site Selection Guidelines

Need for Security Criteria

From a security point of view, proper site selection is the most important initial step to provide adequate protection. It is the intent of this booklet to bring to the attention of all responsible personnel the wide range of security matters that should be addressed and integrated into the site selection process for new office buildings and existing buildings.

Because of car bombings there are new criteria for site selection on a worldwide basis. Regardless of the geographic process, thereby preparing for what might happen during the life of the building or its occupancy. We have all seen how quickly a benign security situation can evolve into a significant threat to facilities. It is only prudent to incorporate adequate security measures based on an evaluation of the existing threat and the potential for a higher future threat level to protect your employees and visitors for the long term. It will be evident from the factors highlighted that security considerations will impact on operational matters. The implication of this fact may be greater in some geographic regions than in others and will certainly affect some more seriously than others. Where this is the case, it is incumbent on all interested parties to evaluate potential damage while engaged in the site selection process and balance it against security requirements.

If, in high threat areas, many of the suggested key criteria cannot be met the firm should consider choosing another, more secure location.

Everyone involved in site selections should be aware of the following suggested criteria for facilities.

New Office Building

Topography

Site ideally should be situated at the high point, if any, of a land tract, which makes it less vulnerable to weapons fire, makes egress/ingress more difficult and easier to detect or observe any intrusions.

Siting

Site should be located away from main thoroughfares and provide for the following:

- 100 feet minimum setback from the building to perimeter walls and vehicular entrances to the building.

- Sufficient parking space for personnel outside the compound in a secure area within sight of the building, preferably, immediately adjacent to the compound.

- Sufficient parking space for visitors near the site but not on the site itself.

- Sufficient space to allow for the construction of a vehicular security control checkpoint (lock-type system), which would allow vehicles to be searched, if deemed necessary, and cleared without providing direct access to the site.

- Sufficient space to allow for the construction of a pedestrian security control checkpoint (gatehouse/booth) to check identification, conduct a package check or parcel inspection or carry out visitor processing before the pedestrian is allowed further access to the site. If a need for a thorough check of purses and briefcases, as well as items carried on a person may be required, sufficient space for a Walk-Through Metal Detector (WTMD) should be considered. Walking through a WTMD is less intrusive than a personal search or even one conducted with a hand-held detector.

- Sufficient space for construction of a 9-foot outer perimeter barrier or wall.

Environmental Considerations

Site should be located in a semi-residential, semi-commercial area where local vehicular traffic flow patterns do not impede access to or from the site.

Existing Office Building

The following security considerations for high-rise buildings are listed in order of preference as the availability of local facilities dictate:

- A detached (free-standing) building and site entirely occupied and controlled by you.

- A semidetached office building that is entirely occupied by you.

- A nondetached office building that is entirely occupied and controlled by you.

- A detached (free-standing) office building in which the uppermost floors are entirely occupied and controlled by you.

- A semidetached office building in which the uppermost floors are entirely occupied and controlled by you.

- A nondetached office building in which the uppermost floors are entirely occupied and controlled by you.

- A detached (free-standing) office building in which the central floors are entirely occupied and controlled by you.

- A semidetached office building in which the central floors are entirely occupied and controlled by you.

- A nondetached office building in which the central floors are entirely occupied and controlled by you.

- A detached (free-standing) office building in which some floors are occupied and controlled by you.

- A semidetached office building in which some floors are occupied and controlled by you.

- A nondetached office building in which some floors are occupied and controlled by you.

Common Requirements

Both new and existing office buildings should be capable of accommodating these security items:

- Floor load capacity must be able to maintain the additional weight of public access control (PAC) equipment (ballistic doors, walls, windows), security containers, and disintegrators and shredders, if needed.

- Exterior walls must be smooth shell, sturdy, and protected to a height of 16 feet to prevent forced entry.

- Building must be conducive to grilling or eliminating all windows below 16 feet.

The previously listed criteria should be adopted to provide satisfactory protection for employees and visitors. If the site is found to be deficient in some areas, attempt to resolve those deficiencies by instituting security measures that will negate the deficiencies. Professional security and/or engineering assistance should be considered to address unique situations.

At a minimum, the following general security measures should be incorporated into planning designs: perimeter controls, grillwork, and shatter-resistant film for windows, public access controls, package search and check, secured area, provisions for emergency egress, and emergency alarms and emergency power.

Standards of Design for Site and Building Security

This section establishes the minimum physical security standards to be incorporated in the design of facilities.

The intent is to provide protection for assets, personnel, property, and customers; ensure that consistent security measures are used at various locations; and ensure design integrity and compatibility of all elements of security with the architecture of the site.

Labor-saving and state-of-the-art security system components and assemblies should be used in all U.S. activities operating overseas, provided they can be maintained locally and there are spare parts available locally.

For manufacturing plant and laboratory facilities, security equipment such as closed-circuit television (CCTV) cameras and monitors, intercoms, card readers, and special glass protection, should be considered. Special care should be taken to verify the vendor's references, especially as they pertain to the quality of alarms, a visit should be made to the central station to observe the professionalism of the operation. Design, purchase, and installation should be coordinated through your architect. Bear in mind, and make provisions for, the cost of maintenance on your security equipment. In some locations overseas, security equipment may be less expensive and more reliable than guards who receive relatively low pay and little training.

Security Design Objectives

In designing business or activity sites, roadways, buildings, and interior space, the following functional security objectives should be achieved:

- Physical and psychological boundaries (signs, closed doors, etc.) should establish four areas with increasing security controls beginning at the property boundaries. The areas are defined as:

- perimeter - property boundaries;
- exterior - lobbies/docks;
- interior - employee space; and
- restricted - laboratories, computer rooms, etc.

- Vehicular traffic signs should clearly designate the separate entrances for trucks/deliveries and visitors and employee vehicles. Where feasible control points should be provided near the site boundaries. Sidewalks should channel pedestrians toward controlled lobbies and entrances.

- Avoid having unsecured areas where there is no one nearby with responsibility for the function of the areas.

Chapter III. Exterior Protection

Perimeter Security

Walls, Fences, Berms, etc.

The overall design for perimeter security should consider using natural barriers, fencing, landscaping, or other physical or psychological boundaries to demonstrate a security presence to all site visitors.

If the threat is considered to be high at free-standing facilities, there should be a smooth faced perimeter wall or combination wall/fence, a minimum of 9 feet tall and extending 3 feet below grade. The wall or fence may be constructed of stone, masonry, concrete, chain link, or steel grillwork. However, if space limitations and local conditions dictate the need, any newly constructed wall should be designed to prevent vehicle penetration, and should use a reinforced concrete foundation wall, 18 inches thick with an additional 1-1/2 inches of concrete covering on each side of the steel reinforcement, and extending 36 inches above the grade. This type of wall is designed to support three wall toppings: masonry, concrete, or steel picket fencing. The toppings should be securely anchored into the foundation wall. If a picket fence is used instead of a wall, the upright supports should be spaced at least 9 feet apart so that the fence, if knocked down, cannot be used as a ladder. In addition, intrusion alert systems can be used to enhance perimeter security.

In cases where the above standards of construction are neither feasible, fiscally prudent, nor required by the threat, alternative methods offering comparable protection can be used. These alternatives should maximize the use of locally available materials and conditions to take advantage of existing terrain features or by the creative use of earth berms and landscaping techniques such as concrete planters.

Inside the perimeter barrier, the building should be set back on the property to provide maximum distance from that portion of the perimeter barrier which is accessible by vehicle. The desirable distance of the setback is at least 100 feet depending on the bomb resistance provided by the barrier.

At facilities with less than optimum barriers, or at locations where the terrorist threat or building location increases the vulnerability to vehicular attack, bollards*[1] or cement planters can be used to strengthen the perimeter boundary. At walled or fenced facilities with insufficient setback, bollards or planters can be installed outside the perimeter to increase the setback of the buildings.

(In any event, whether at a walled facility or a nonwalled one as discussed below, the design and placement of bollards or other antivehicular devices

---

[1] A device constructed to protect against a ramming vehicle attack. They are deployed in lines around a perimeter for anti-ram protection, or to provide supplemental control of vehicle traffic through permanent checkpoints when other means are not practical or effective.

should be considered in the early planning stages. It would prevent having impenetrable gates connected by easily penetrated walls, or necessitate relocating because local authorities forbid the construction of required barriers.)

Nonwalled Facilities Barriers

In locations without perimeter wall protection, buildings should be protected with bollards, cement planters, or any other perimeter protection device. Such devices should be placed in a manner as to allow the maximum distance between the building and the roadway and/or vehicle access area. They should be positioned to impede vehicular access to lobbies and other glassed areas that could be penetrated by a vehicle (i.e., low or no curb, glass wall or door structure between lobby and driveway). Driveways should be designed and constructed to minimize or preclude high-speed vehicular approaches to lobbies and glassed areas. (There may be local ordinances that make placement of these devices illegal or ineffective.)

A positive and concerted effort should be made to contact local host country law enforcement or governmental authorities and request that they prohibit, restrict, or impede motor vehicles from parking, stopping, or loading in front of the facility.

In high threat locations, if local conditions or government officials prohibit antivehicular perimeter security measures and your business is either the sole occupant of the building or located on the first or second floor, you should consider relocating to more secure facilities.

Building Exterior

Facade

The building exterior should be a sheer/smooth shell, devoid of footholds, decorative lattice work, ledges, or balconies. The building facade should be protected to a height of 16 feet to prevent access by intruders using basic hand tools. The use of glass on the building facade should be kept to an absolute minimum, only being used for standard size or smaller windows and, possibly, main entrance doors. All glass should be protected by plastic film. Consider the use of lexan or other polycarbonate as alternatives to glass where practical.

External Doors

Local fire codes may impact on the guidance presented here. As decisions are made on these issues, local fire codes will have to be considered.

Main entrance doors may be either transparent or opaque and constructed of wood, metal, or glass. The main entrance door should be equipped with a double-cylinder dead bolt and additionally secured with crossbar or sliding dead bolts attached vertically to the top and bottom of each leaf. All doors, including interior doors, should be installed to take advantage of the doorframe strength by having the doors open toward the attack side.

All other external doors should be opaque hollow metal fire doors with no external hardware. These external doors should be single doors unless used for delivery and loading purposes.

Should double doors be required, they should be equipped with two sliding dead bolts on the active leaf and two sliding dead bolts on the inactive leaf vertically installed on the top and bottom of the doors. A local alarmed panic bar and a 180-degree peephole viewing device should be installed on the active leaf.

All external doors leading to crawl spaces or basements must be securely padlocked and regularly inspected for tampering.

Windows

The interior side of all glass surfaces should be covered with a protective plastic film that meets or exceeds the manufacturer's specifications for shatter-resistant protective film. A good standard is 4-millimeter thickness for all protective film applications. This film will keep glass shards to a minimum in the event of an explosion or if objects are thrown through the window.

Grillwork should be installed on all exterior windows and air-conditioning units that are within 16 feet of grade or are accessible from roofs, balconies, etc. The rule of thumb here is to cover all openings in excess of 100 square inches if the smallest dimension is 6 inches or larger.

Grillwork should be constructed of 1/2-inch diameter or greater steel rebar, anchored or imbedded (not bolted) into the window frame or surrounding masonry to a depth of 3 inches. Grillwork should be installed horizontally and vertically on center at no more than 8-inch intervals. However, grillwork installed in exterior window frames within the secure area should be spaced 5 inches on center, horizontally and vertically, and anchored in the manner described previously. Decorative grillwork patterns can be used for aesthetic purposes.

Grillwork that is covering windows designated as necessary for emergency escape should be hinged for easy egress. All hinged grillwork should be secured with a key operated security padlock. The key should be maintained on a cup hook in close proximity of the hinged grille, but out of reach of an intruder. These emergency escape windows should not be used in planning for fire evacuations.

Roof

The roof should be constructed of fire-resistant material. All hatches and doors leading to the roof should be securely locked with dead-bolt locks. Security measures such as barbed, concertina or tape security wire, broken glass, and walls or fences may be used to prevent access from nearby trees and/or adjoining roofs.

Vehicular Entrance and Controls

Vehicular Entrance

Vehicular entry-exit points should be kept to a minimum. Ideally, to maximize traffic flow and security, only two regularly used vehicular entry-exit points are necessary. Both should be similarly constructed and monitored. The use of one would be limited to employees' cars, while the other would be used by visitors and delivery vehicles. Depending on the size and nature of the facility, a gate for emergency vehicular and pedestrian egress should be installed at a location that is easily and safely accessible by employees. Emergency gates should be securely locked and periodically checked. All entry-exit points should be secured with a heavy-duty sliding steel, iron, or heavily braced chain link gate equipped with a heavy locking device.

The primary gate should be electrically operated (with a manual back-up by a security officer situated in an adjacent booth). The gate at the vehicle entrance should be positioned to avoid a long straight approach to force approaching vehicles to slow down before reaching the gate. The general technique employed is to require a sharp turn immediately in front of the gate.

In addition to the gate, and whenever justifiable, a vehicular arrest system can be installed. An appropriate vehicle arrest system, whether active, a piece of equipment designed to stop vehicles in their tracks, or passive, a dense mass, will be able to stop or instantly disable a vehicle with a minimum gross weight of 15,000 pounds traveling 50 miles per hour.

Vehicular Control

General

All facilities should have some method of vehicle access control. Primary road entrances to all major plant, laboratory, and office locations should have a vehicle control facility capable of remote operation by security personnel with automated systems.

- At smaller facilities, vehicle access control may be provided by badge-activated gates, manual swing gates, etc.

- Site security should be able to close all secondary road entrances thereby limiting access to the primary entrance. Lighting and turn space should be provided as appropriate.

Control Features

Primary perimeter entrances to a facility should have a booth for security personnel during peak traffic periods and automated systems for remote operations during other periods.

Capabilities are:

- Electrically-operated gates to be activated by security personnel at either the booth or security control center or by a badge reader located in a convenient location for a driver;

- CCTV with the capability of displaying full-facial features of a driver and vehicle characteristics on the monitor at security control center;

- An intercom system located in a convenient location for a driver to communicate with the gatehouse and security control center;

- Bollards or other elements to protect the security booth and gates against car crash;

- Sensors to activate the gate, detect vehicles approaching and departing the gate, activate a CCTV monitor displaying the gate, sound an audio alert in the security control center;

- Lighting to illuminate the gate area and approaches to a higher level than surrounding areas;

- Signs to instruct visitors and to post property as required;

- Road surfaces to enable queuing, turnaround, and parking;

- Vehicle bypass control (i.e., gate extensions), low and dense shrubbery, fences, and walls.

Booth Construction and Operation

As noted previously, at the perimeter vehicular entry-exit a security officer booth should be constructed to control access. (At facilities not having perimeter walls, the security officer booth should be installed immediately inside the facility foyer.)
If justified by the threat level the security officer booth should be completely protected with reinforced concrete, walls, ballistic doors, and windows. The booth should be equipped with a security officer duress alarm and intercom system, both annunciating at the facility receptionist and security officer's office. This security officer would also be responsible for complete operation of the vehicle gate. If necessary, package inspection and visitor screening may be conducted just outside of the booth by an unarmed security officer equipped with walk-through and hand-held metal detectors. Provisions for the

environmental comfort should be considered when designing the booth.

Parking

General

Security should be considered in the location and arrangement of parking lots. Pedestrians leaving parking lots should be channeled toward a limited number of building entrances.

All parking facilities should have an emergency communication system (intercom, telephones, etc.) installed at strategic locations to provide emergency communications directly to Security.

Parking lots should be provided with CCTV cameras capable of displaying and videotaping lot activity on a monitor in the security control center. Lighting must be of adequate level and direction to support cameras while, at the same time, giving consideration to energy efficiency and local environmental concerns.

If possible, parking on streets directly adjacent to the building should be forbidden. Wherever justifiable given the threat profile of your company, there should be no underground parking areas in the neither building basement nor ground-level parking under building overhangs.

Within Perimeter Walls/Fences

All parking within perimeter walls or fences should be restricted to employees, with spaces limited to an area as far from the building as possible. Parking for patrons and visitors, except for predesignated VIP visitors, should be restricted to outside of the perimeter wall/fences.

Garages

For those buildings having an integral parking garage or structure, a complete system for vehicle control should be provided. CCTV surveillance should be provided for employee safety and building security. If the threat of car bombing is extant, consideration must be given to prohibiting parking in the building.

Access from the garage or parking structure into the building should be limited, secure, well lighted, and have no places of concealment. Elevators, stairs, and connecting bridges serving the garage or parking structure should discharge into a staffed or fully monitored area. Convex mirrors should be mounted outside the garage elevators to reflect the area adjacent to the door openings.

Exterior Lighting

Exterior lighting should illuminate all facility entrances and exits in addition to parking areas, perimeter walls, gates, courtyards, garden areas, and shrubbery rows.

Lighting of building exterior and walkways should be provided where required for employee safety and security. Regarding building facades, there should be a capability to illuminate them 100% to a height of at least 6 feet.

Although sodium vapor lights are considered optimum for security purposes, the use of incandescent and florescent light fixtures is adequate. Exterior fixtures should be protected with grillwork when theft or vandalism have been identified as a problem.

For leased buildings, landlord approval of exterior lighting design requirements should be included in lease agreements.

Building Access

Building Entrances

The number of building entrances should be minimized, relative to the site, building layout, and functional requirements. A single off-hours entrance near the security control center is desirable. At large sites, additional secured entrances should be considered with provisions for monitoring and control.

Door Security Requirements

- All employee entrance doors should permit installation of controlled access system hardware. The doors, jambs, hinges and locks must be designed to resist forced entry (e.g., spreading of door frames, accessing panic hardware, shimming bolts and/or latches, fixed hinge pins). Don't forget handicap requirements when applicable.

- Minimum requirement for lock cylinders are "6-pin" pin-tumbler-type. Locks with removable core cylinders to permit periodic changing of the locking mechanism should be used.

- All exterior doors should have alarm sensors to detect unauthorized openings.

- Doors designed specifically for emergency exits need to have an alarm that is audible at the door with an additional annunciation at the security control center. These doors should have no exterior hardware on them.

Window Precautions

- For protection, large showroom type plate glass and small operable windows on the ground floor should be avoided. If, however, these types of windows are used and the building is located in a high-risk area, special consideration should be given to the use of locking and alarm devices, laminated glass, wire glass, film, or polycarbonate glazing.

- For personnel protection, all windows should have shatter-resistant film.

- (For a more extensive discussion of windows and how to secure them, as well as guidance for securing windows which may be used for emergency exit, see "Windows" on page 9).

Lobby

Main entrances to buildings should have space for a receptionist during the day and a security officer at night. The security control center should be located adjacent to the main entrance lobby and should be surrounded by professionally designed protective materials.

The lobby-reception area should be a single, self-sufficient building entrance. Telephones and rest rooms to meet the needs of the public should be provided in this area without requiring entry into interior space. Rest rooms should be kept locked in high-threat environments and access controlled by the receptionist.

Consistent with existing risk level, the receptionist should not be allowed to accept small parcel or courier deliveries routinely unless they are expected by addressee.

Other Building Access Points

Other less obvious points of building entry, such as grilles, grating, manhole covers, areaways, utility tunnels, mechanical wall, and roof penetrations should be protected to impede and/or prevent entry into the building.

Permanent exterior stairs or ladders from the ground floor to the roof should not be used, nor should the building facade allow a person to climb up unaided. Exterior fire escapes should be retractable and secured in the up position.

Construction Activities

Landscaping and other outside architectural and/or aesthetic features should minimize creating any area that could conceal a person in close proximity to walkways, connecting links, buildings, and recreational spaces.

Landscaping design should include CCTV surveillance of building approaches and parking areas.

Landscape plantings around building perimeters need to be located at a minimum of 4 feet from the building wall to prevent concealing of people or objects.

Chapter IV. Interior Protection

Building Layout

Building space can be divided into three categories: public areas, interior areas, and security or restricted areas requiring special security measures. These areas should be separated from one another within the building with a limited number of controlled passage points between the areas. "Controlled" in this context can allow or deny passage by any means deemed necessary (i.e., locks, security officers, etc.).

Corridors, stairwells, and other accessible areas should be arranged to avoid places for concealment.

Generally, restricted space should be located above the ground-floor level, away from exterior walls, and away from hazardous operations. Access to restricted space should be allowed only from interior space and not from exterior or public areas. Exit routes for normal or emergency egress should not transit restricted or security space.

Walls and Partitions

Public space should be separated from interior space and restricted space by slab-to-slab partitions. When the area above a hung ceiling is used as a common air return, provide appropriate modifications to walls or install alarm sensors. In shared occupancy buildings, space should be separated by slab-to-slab construction or as described previously.

Doors

Normally, interior doors do not require special features or provisions for locking.

In shared occupancy buildings, every door leading to interior space should be considered an exterior door and designed with an appropriate degree of security.

Stairway doors located in multitenant buildings must be secured from the stairwell side (local fire regulations permitting) and always operable from the office side. In the event that code prevents these doors from being secured, the floor plan should be altered to provide security to your space.

Emergency exit doors that are designed specifically for that purpose should be equipped with a local audible alarm at the door and a signal at the monitoring location.

Doors to restricted access areas should be designed to resist intrusion and accommodate controlled-access hardware and alarms.

Doors on building equipment and utility rooms, electric closets, and telephone rooms should be provided with locks having a removable core, as is provided on exterior doors. As a minimum requirement, provide 6-pin tumbler locks.

For safety reasons, door hardware on secured interior doors should permit exit by means of a single knob or panic bar.

Other Public Areas

The design of public areas should prevent concealment of unauthorized personnel and/or objects.

Ceilings in lobbies, rest rooms, and similar public areas should be made inaccessible with securely fastened or locked access panels installed where necessary to service equipment.

Public rest rooms and elevator lobbies in shared occupancy buildings should have ceilings that satisfy your security requirements.

Special Storage Requirements

Building vaults or metal safes may be required to protect cash or negotiable documents, precious metals, classified materials, etc. Vault construction should be made of reinforced concrete or masonry and be resistant to fire damage. Steel vault doors are available with various fire-related and security penetration classifications.

Elevators

All elevators should have emergency communications and emergency lighting. In shared occupancy buildings, elevators traveling to your interior space should be equipped with badge readers or other controls to prohibit unauthorized persons from direct entry into your interior space. If this is not feasible, a guard, receptionist or other means of access control may be necessary at each entry point.

Cable Runs

All cable termination points, terminal blocks, and/or junction boxes should be within your space. Where practical, enclose cable runs in steel conduit.

Cables passing through space that you do not control should be continuous and installed in conduit. You might even want to install an alarm in the conduit. Junction boxes should be minimized and fittings spot welded when warranted.

Security Monitoring

Security Control Center

If you have a security control center, it should have adequate space for security personnel and their equipment. Additional office space for technicians and managers should be available adjacent to the control center.

Your security control center should provide a fully integrated console designed to optimize the operator's ability to receive and evaluate security information and initiate appropriate response actions for (1) access control, (2) CCTV, (3) life safety, (4) intrusion and panic alarm, (5) communications, and (6) fully zoned public address system control.

The control center should have emergency power and convenient toilet facilities. Lighting should avoid glare on TV monitors and computer terminals. Sound-absorbing materials should be used on floors, walls, and ceilings. All security power should be backed up by an emergency electrical system.

The control center should be protected to the same degree as the most secure area it monitors.

Controlled Access System

This type of system, if used, should include the computer hardware, monitoring station terminals, sensors, badge readers, door control devices, and the necessary communication links (leased line, digital dialer, or radio transmission) to the computer.

In addition to the normal designated access control system's doors and/or gates, remote access control points should interface to the following systems: (1) CCTV, (2) intercom, and (3) door and/or gate release.

Alarm Systems

Sensors should be resistant to surreptitious bypass. Door contact monitor switches should be recessed wherever possible. Surface-mounted contact switches should have protective covers.

Intrusion and fire alarms for restricted areas should incorporate a backup battery power supply and be on circuits energized by normal and emergency generator power.

Control boxes, external bells, and junction boxes for all alarm systems should be secured with high-quality locks and electrically wired to cause an alarm if opened.

Alarm systems should be fully multiplexed in large installations. Alarm systems should interface with the computer-based security system and CCTV system.

Security sensors should individually register an audio-visual alarm (annunciator or computer, if provided) located at the security central monitoring location and alert the security officer. A single-CRT display should have a redundant printer or indicator light. A hard-wired audible alarm that meets common fire code standards should be activated with distinguishing characteristics for fire, intrusion, emergency exit, etc. All alarms ought to be locked in until reset manually.

Closed-Circuit TV (CCTV)

CCTV systems should permit the observation of multiple camera transmission images from one or more remote locations.

Switching equipment should be installed to permit the display of any camera on any designated monitor.

Hardware

To ensure total system reliability, only high-quality security hardware should be integrated into the security system.

Stairwell Door Reentry System

In multitenant high-rise facilities, stairwell doors present a potential security problem. These doors must be continuously operable from the office side into the stairwells. Reentry should be controlled to permit only authorized access and prevent entrapment in the stairwell.

Reentry problems can be fixed if you provide locks on all stairwell doors except the doors leading to the first floor (lobby level) and approximately every fourth or fifth floor, or as required by local fire code requirements. Doors without these locks should be fitted with sensors to transmit alarms to the central security monitoring location and provide an audible alarm at the door location. Appropriate signs should be placed within the stairwells. Doors leading to roofs should be secured to the extent permitted by local fire code.

Special Functional Requirements

Facilities with unique functions may have special security requirements in addition to those stated in this booklet. These special requirements should be discussed with Corporate Security personnel or a security consultant. Typical areas with special requirements are product centers, parts distribution centers; sensitive parts storage facilities, customer centers, service exchange centers, etc.

Chapter V. Public Access Controls (PAC)

Security Officers and Watchmen

All facilities of any size in threatened locations should have manned 24-hour internal protection. Security Officers should be uniformed personnel and, if possible, placed under contract. They should be thoroughly trained, bilingual and have complete instructions in their native language clearly outlining their duties and responsibilities. These instructions should also be printed in English for the benefit of

American supervisory personnel. If permitted by local law/customs, investigations or checks into the backgrounds of security officers should be conducted.

At facilities with a perimeter wall, there should be one 24-hour perimeter security officer post. If the facility maintains a separate vehicular entrance security officer post, such a post should be manned from 1 hour before to 1 hour after normal business hours and during special events. Security officers should be responsible for conducting package inspections, package check-in, and, if used, should operate the walk-through and hand-held metal detectors. Security officers should also be responsible for inspecting local and international mail delivered to the facility, both visually and with a hand-held metal detector before it is distributed. X-ray equipment for package inspection should be employed if the level of risk dictates.

At facilities with a perimeter guardhouse, the walk-through metal detector could be maintained and operated in an unsecured pass-through portion of the guardhouse. In addition, this security officer could also be responsible for conducting package inspections. When there is sufficient room to store packages at the guardhouse, checked packages should be stored here--new guardhouses should provide for such storage. If package storage at the guardhouse is not feasible, then it should be in shelves in the foyer under the direction of the foyer security officer or receptionist. Generally, security screening and package storage is carried out in the foyer.

Security Hardline

Office areas should be equipped with a "hardline" to provide physical protection from unregulated public access. Protection should be provided by a forced-entry-resistant hardline that meets ballistic protection standards. These standards can be obtained from your corporate personnel or a security consultant. When a security hardline for Public Access Control (PAC) is constructed, the following criteria should apply:

Walls

Walls comprising a PAC should be constructed of no less than 6 inches of reinforced concrete from slab to slab. The reinforcement should be of at least Number 5 rebar spaced 5 inches on center, horizontally and vertically, and anchored in both slabs. In existing buildings, the following are acceptable substitutions for 5-inch reinforced concrete hardlines:

- Solid masonry, 6 inches thick or greater, with reinforcing bars horizontally and vertically installed;

- Solid unreinforced masonry or brick, 8 inches thick or greater;

- Hollow masonry block, 4 to 8 inches thick with 1/4-inch steel backing;

- Solid masonry, at least 6 inches thick, with 1/4-inch steel backing;

- Fabricated ballistic steel wall, using two 1/4-inch layers of sheet steel separated by tubular steel studs;

- Reinforced concrete, less than 6 inches thick with 1/8-inch steel backing.

Security Doors

Either opaque or transparent security doors can be used for PAC doors. All doors should provide a 15-minute forced entry penetration delay. In addition, doors should be ballistic resistant.

The PAC door should be a local access control door, meaning a receptionist or security officer can remotely open the door.

Security Windows

Whenever a security window or teller-window is installed in the hardline, it should meet the 15-minute forced entry and standard ballistic resistance requirements.

PAC Entry Requirements

No visitor should be allowed to enter through the hardline without being visually identified by a security officer, receptionist, or other employee stationed behind the hardline. If the identity of the visitor cannot be established, the visitor must be escorted at all times while in the facility.

Alarms and Intercoms

A telephone intercom between the secure office area, the foyer security officer, and guardhouse should be installed. In facilities where deemed necessary, a central alarm and public address system should be installed to alert staff and patrons of an emergency situation. Where such a system is required, the primary control console should be located in the security control center. Keep in mind that alarms without emergency response plans may be wasted alarms. Design, implement, and practice emergency plans.

Secure Area

Every facility should be equipped with a secure area for immediate use in an emergency situation. This area is not intended to be used for prolonged periods of time. In the event of emergency, employees will vacate the premises as soon as possible. The secure area, therefore, is provided for the immediate congregation of employees at which time emergency exit plans would be implemented.

The secure area should be contained within the staff office area, behind the established hardline segregating offices from public access. An individual office will usually be designated as the secure area. Entrance into the secure area should be protected by a solid core wood or hollow metal door equipped with two sliding dead bolts.

Emergency egress from the secure area will be through an opaque 15 minute forced-entry-resistant door equipped with an alarmed panic bar or through a grilled window, hinged for emergency egress. The exit preferably will not be visible from the facility's front entrance.

Chapter VI. Emergency Exit

All facilities should have a means of emergency escape aside from the secure area exit. Positioned appropriately throughout the building should be sufficient emergency exit points to accommodate normal facility occupancy.

All emergency doors should be hollow metal doors (fire doors where appropriate) equipped with alarmed emergency exit panic bars.

Emergency factors regarding windows are described in Chapter III.

Chapter VII. Communications

Communications Facilities

Satellite ground stations, microwave parabolic reflectors, and communications towers and supports should be located on rooftops, with limited access to the public. Where this is not possible, the equipment should be installed with fences and alarms. Closed circuit television (CCTV) with video recording capability should be considered and included where justified.

Communications

Telephone systems should incorporate an external direct line telephone link for security and life safety independent of the internal telephone network dedicated to the location. This line should feed into the secure area.

Communications considerations should provide radio transmission equipment for communications between security personnel.

Intercom systems should have the capacity to accommodate all remote access control points.

Systems Integration

Security systems in new buildings or buildings undergoing renovation should be installed with distributed wiring schemes that use local telecommunication closets as distribution points. This will provide expansion capability, future networking capability, ease of maintenance, and full function implementation of the security system. At a minimum, the communications link and interface between the sensor, output devices, and computers should include conduit, multiconductor twisted shielded cable and terminal cabinets. However, recent technology such as fiber-optic cables should be considered in planning the wiring distribution scheme. Data distribution and gathering closets used for security wiring must be secure. Where possible, integrate security wiring with other systems such as telephone, paging, energy management, etc. In every case, the design of the communications link should permit ready installation and interconnection of cameras, sensors, and other input-output devices. All life safety equipment and accessories should be Underwriters Laboratory (UL) approved.

Outlying facilities should link security systems to the nearest security control center. All new systems should be compatible with existing systems or the existing system should be replaced with the new system.

Chapter VIII. Office Security Guidelines

General Procedures

Any employee, but especially the executive, can be a target of terrorist or criminal tactics and forced entry, building occupation, kidnapping, sabotage, and even assassination. Executive offices can be protected against attacks.

The executive office should have a physical barrier such as electromagnetically operated doors, a silent trouble alarm button, with a signal terminating in the Plant Protection Department or at the secretary's desk, and close screening of visitors at the reception and security officer desks in the lobbies and again at the executive's office itself. Secretaries should not admit visitors unless positively screened in advance or known from previous visits. If the visitor is not known and/or not expected, he or she should not be admitted until satisfactory identification and a valid reason to be on site is established. In such instances, Security should be called and an officer asked to come to the scene until the visitor establishes a legitimate reason for being in the office. If the visitor cannot do so, the officer should be asked to escort the visitor out of the building.

Unusual telephone calls, particularly those in which the caller does not identify himself/herself or those in which it appears that the caller may be misrepresenting himself/herself, should not be put through to the executive. Note should be made of the circumstances involved (i.e., incoming line number, date and time, nature of call, name of caller). This information should then be provided to the Security Department for follow-up investigation.

Under no circumstances should an executive's secretary reveal to unknown callers the whereabouts of the executive, his/her home address, or telephone number.

The executive, when working alone in the evening, on weekends, or holidays, should advise Security how long he/she will be in the office and check out with Security when leaving.

Security in the Office

American enterprises, particularly those in foreign countries, have been and will continue to be the subject of controversial political and economic issues that can turn their executives and offices into targets for terrorists and criminal actions. Countermeasures against these acts can and should be implemented in the office environment. The following list describes some of the measures that may be useful in improving personal security and safety at the office.

- Avoid working alone late at night and on days when the remainder of the staff is absent.

- The office door should be locked when you vacate your office for any lengthy period, at night and on weekends. Do not permit the secretary to leave keys to the office or desk.

- There should be limited access to the executive office area.

- Arrange office interiors so that strange or foreign objects left in the room will be immediately recognized.

- Unescorted visitors should not be allowed admittance nor should workmen without proper identification and authorization.

- Implement a clean desk policy. Do not leave papers nor travel plans on desk tops unattended.

- Control publicity in high-risk areas. Avoid identification by photographs for news release. Maintain a low profile.

- Janitorial or maintenance activity in key offices and factory areas should be supervised by competent company employees.

- A fire extinguisher, first-aid kit, and oxygen bottle should be stored in the office area.

- The most effective physical security configuration is to have doors locked (from within) with one visitor access door to the office area.

- Where large numbers of employees are involved, use the identification badge system containing a photograph.

Advice for Secretaries

A secretary has close knowledge of schedules and company business. He/she should be instructed to maximize security, and the following precautionary measures should be reviewed with him/her:

- Be alert to strangers visiting the executive without an appointment and who are unknown to him/her.

- Be alert to strangers who loiter near the office.

- Do not reveal the executive's whereabouts to unknown callers. Even if the caller is known, the information should be on a need-to-know basis. As a standard policy, take a number where the caller can be contacted. Do not give out home telephone numbers or addresses.

- When receiving a threatening call, including a bomb threat, extortion threat, or from a mentally disturbed individual, remain calm and listen carefully. Each secretary and/or receptionist should have a threatening telephone call checklist which should be completed as soon as possible.

- Keep executive travel and managers' travel itineraries confidential. Strictly limit distribution to those with a need to know.

- Incinerate, disintegrate or shred notes, drafts, correspondence and any and all material which reveal an executive's travel plans, itineraries, home address and telephone number, invitations and responses thereto or any other data about his/her whereabouts, including information about past trips which could indicate habitual contacts and travel patterns. Do not place such material in trash cans.

- Observe caution when opening mail. A list of things to look for is included in Appendix IV. You should post this list in your mail handling facility. (All persons handling mail should be made aware of the aforementioned basic signs found in Appendix IV. The mail handlers should have available an established procedure in the event that any of the above signs are found. It is also important not to accept packages from strangers until satisfied with the individual's identity and the nature of the parcel.)

Precautions for All

Money, valuables, and important papers such as passports should not be kept in your desk. Thefts will occur in all offices, even during working hours. Some will be solved; most could have been prevented. The following suggestions will decrease the chance of further thefts:

- Do not tempt thieves by leaving valuables or money unsecured.

- If sharing an office or suite of offices, stagger lunch hours and coffee breaks so that the office is occupied at all times.

- If the office must be left vacant, lock the door.

- Locate desks in a way that persons entering the office or suite can be observed.

- Follow a clean desk policy before leaving at night. Keep valuables and company documents in locked containers.

- Confirm work to be done or property to be removed by Maintenance, outside service personnel, or vendors.

- Do not "hide" keys to office furniture under flower pots, calendars, etc. Thieves know all the hiding places. Do not label keys except by code.

Chapter IX. Vehicular and Travel Security

Vehicle and Travel Security

Threats of terrorism and kidnapping are serious problems involving all aspects of security management; effective management dictates that available resources be used wisely and concentrated on security weak points. Terrorists are very quick to identify the security vulnerabilities of business, family, and pleasure travel. At their best, protection strategies dealing with vehicles and travel are perhaps the hardest to formulate, and the advantage tends to be with the terrorist. Current statistics indicate that the greatest danger from acts of terrorism occurs while the executive is traveling to or from the office and just before reaching his/her destination.

The inherent security problems of passenger vehicle travel are many. Vehicles are easily recognized by year, make, and model, and the trained terrorist can accurately assess any protection modifications and security devices. Using adequate resources, vehicles can be discreetly followed; therefore, making possible repeated dry runs of potential attacks with very low risk of detection. Under these conditions, different methods of attack can be formulated and tested until success is ensured. While traveling in a passenger vehicle, the executive has limited protection resources upon which to rely and often is dependent on fixed security manpower. This makes it easier for terrorist groups, which are geared to mobility, to ensure numerical superiority.

The attack potential against the executive in travel rests heavily on psychological instability and human weakness. The shock of surprise attack is greatest at points of changing surroundings, crossroads, and when entering or exiting vehicles. These are situations of constant change and points of activity where the executive has a tendency to be mentally off balance. Vehicles are often left in driveways, on streets, at service centers, and other isolated areas with no form of control or protection, allowing easy access to terrorists. Through illegal entry to the vehicle, the terrorist can gain a number of attack points; sabotage with the intent to maim and injure, sabotage with the intent of execution, and sabotage to ensure the success of future attacks. These psychological factors make the vehicle the ideal place to apply scare tactics, warnings, and gain initial control of the executive.

Even though travel problems provide the greatest number of security and psychological variables, there are actions and policies that can be developed to minimize the executive's risk and complicate the terrorist's plans. The basic travel policy can be divided into three areas: (1) Normal Travel Procedures, (2) Vehicle Equipment, and (3) Vehicle Defense Strategy. The following checklists will aid in formulating and evaluating an effective travel security policy.

Normal Travel Procedures Checklist

- The avoidance of routine times and patterns of travel by executives is the least expensive security strategy that can be utilized. The selection of the route should be at the discretion of the executive, not of the chauffeur. Always restrict travel plans to a need-to-know basis.

- Avoid driving in remote areas after dark and keep to established, well-traveled roads.

- In high-risk areas or when individuals are considered attractive targets, consideration should be given to executives and drivers being trained in antiterrorism strategy and defensive driving. Establish responsibilities and develop contingency plans.

- There should be a simple duress procedure established between the executive and drivers. Any oral or visual signal will suffice (i.e., something that the executive or driver says or does only if something is amiss).

- Never overload a vehicle, and all persons should wear seat belts.

- Always park vehicles in parking areas that are either locked or watched and never park overnight on the street. Before entering vehicles, check for signs of tampering.

- When using a taxi service, vary the company. Ensure that the identification photo on the license matches the driver. If uneasy for any reason, simply take another taxi.

- When attending social functions, go with others, if possible.

- Avoid driving close behind other vehicles, especially service trucks, and be aware of activities and road conditions two to three blocks ahead.

- Keep the ignition key separate and never leave the trunk key with parking or service attendants.

- Before each trip, the vehicle should be inspected to see that (1) the hood latch is secure, (2) the fender wells are empty, (3) the exhaust pipe is not blocked, (4) no one is in the back seat or on the floor, and (5) the gas tank is at least three quarters full.

- Establish a firm policy regarding the carrying and use of firearms. Local laws may prohibit firearms.

Vehicle Equipment Checklist

- The executive vehicle designed to meet the terrorist or criminal threat in a high threat area should be a hardtop model with the following special equipment: (1) inside hood latch, (2) locked gas caps, (3) inner escape latch on trunk, (4) steel-belted radial tires with inner tire devices that permit movement even with a flat tire, (5) radiator protection, (6) disk brakes, and (7) an anti-bomb bolt through the end of the exhaust pipe.

- Positive communications can be ensured with a two-way radio or a car telephone.

- It is recommended that the executive vehicle designed to meet the terrorist or criminal threat carry the following safety equipment: (1) fire extinguisher, (2) first-aid kit, (3) flashlight, (4) two spare tires, (5) large outside mirrors, and (6) a portable high-intensity spotlight.

- For additional protection, the vehicle should have an alarm system with an independent power source (an additional battery).

Vehicle Defense Strategy Checklist

- Always be alert to possible surveillance; if followed, drive to the nearest safe location, such as police stations, fire stations, or shopping center and ask for help. Carry a mini-cassette recorder in the car to dictate details of a suspect surveillance car such as color, make, model, license plate, description of occupants, etc. It is difficult to make such detailed notes while driving.

- Where feasible, drive in the inner lanes to keep from being forced to the curb.

- Beware of minor accidents that could block traffic in suspect areas; especially crossroads because they are preferred areas for terrorist or criminal activities as crossroads offer escape advantages.

- If a roadblock is encountered, use shoulder or curb (hit at 30–45-degree angle) to go around, or ram the terrorist or criminal-blocking vehicle. In all cases, do not stop and never allow the executive's vehicle to be boxed in with a loss of maneuverability.

- Blocking vehicles should be rammed in a non-engine area, at 45 degrees, in low gear, and at a constant moderate speed. KNOCK THE BLOCKING VEHICLE OUT OF THE WAY.

- Whenever a target vehicle veers away from the terrorist vehicle, it gives adverse maneuvering room and presents a better target to gunfire.

Travel Security Suggestions

The following are general traveling security suggestions:

- Discuss travel plans on a need-to-know basis only. Telephone operators and secretaries should not advise callers and visitors when an executive is out of town on a trip.

- Remove company logos from luggage. Luggage identification tags should be of a type that allows the information on the tag to be covered. Use the business address on the tag.

- Do not leave valuables and/or sensitive documents in the hotel room.

- When sightseeing, observe basic security precautions and refrain from walking alone in known high-crime areas.

- Always have telephone change available and know how to use the phones. Learn key emergency phrases of the country to be able to ask for police, medical, etc.

- Joggers should carry identification.

- Men should carry wallets either in an inside jacket pocket or a front pants pocket, never in a hip pocket. The less money carried the better. Credit cards can be used for most purchases.

- The telephone numbers of the U.S. Embassy or U.S. Consulate, and company employee contact numbers should be carried with employees at all times.

- Always carry the appropriate documentation for the country being visited.

- When traveling, ask for a hotel room between the second and seventh floors. Most fire department equipment does not reach higher to effect rescue and ground floor rooms are more vulnerable to terrorist or criminal activity.

- American-type hotels usually offer a higher level of safety and security inasmuch as they offer smoke alarms, fire extinguishers, safety locks, hotel security, 24-hour operators, English-speaking personnel, safety deposit boxes, and normally will not divulge a guest's room number.

- Choose taxis carefully and at random. Be sure it is a licensed taxi. Do not use independent non-licensed operators.

- Be as inconspicuous as possible in dress, social activities, and amount of money spent on food, souvenirs, gifts, etc.

- Stay in or use VIP rooms or security zones when waiting in commercial airports abroad. Minimize the amount of time spent in airports.

- Confirm arrivals at destinations with office and/or family. Use an itinerary when traveling.

- When traveling internationally, keep all medicine in original containers and take a copy of the prescription.

Chapter X. Visiting Personnel Protection

General Principles

This chapter provides guidelines regarding security procedures to be implemented during visits of company executives. Guidelines for three levels of threat (minimal threat, moderate threat and high threat) are set forth below along with the factors which determine the level of threat that may exist.

These guidelines should be viewed as tools to assist in organizing and planning visits by company executives or other key personnel. Their implementation will reduce the executive's exposure to terrorist acts, criminal activity, and potential embarrassment.

Minimal Threat-Factors and Guidelines

Minimal Threat Factors

Factors which should be used by management in determining whether in view of the local security environment a minimal threat potential exists include the following:

- A stable local government;

- Effective law enforcement;

- No significant history of terrorist acts against multinational companies or their executives;

- No previous history of criminal or terrorist acts directed against company executives;

- No significant level of criminal activity (particularly violent crimes such as robbery, kidnapping, murder, and rape);

- No current adverse publicity against the company and no local group activity protesting company policies;

- Other risk factors applicable to the local environment.

Minimal Threat Guidelines

Security Coordination

A management-level employee should be assigned as security coordinator. The coordinator's responsibilities consist of implementing the established security guidelines, coordinating all other security aspects of the visit, and serving as the visitor's main contact.

The coordinator should be present at the airport, hotel, and events during arrivals and departures. He/she should ensure adequate security precautions are taken and be present at large public functions.

Air Travel

- Travel in corporate aircraft is preferable because contact with the general public is limited, but use of commercial airlines is an acceptable alternative provided the airline involved is not considered a likely terrorist target.

- When booking reservations, you should make no reference to the visitor's position.

- Personnel should be available at the airport to handle baggage and expedite customs clearances and local airport formalities, both on arrival and departure. A VIP room should be reserved at the airport for possible use in the event of a delayed departure by the aircraft.

- Time spent at the airport should be kept to a minimum. Public areas should be avoided, if at all possible.

- Use of public transportation to and from airports is not recommended.

- Distribution of travel itineraries should be restricted.

Aircraft Security

This section applies in the event that corporate aircraft are used.

- The hiring of contract security officers at major international airports to secure the corporate aircraft during stopovers is not necessary provided that the airport has a viable security system.

- The use of contract security officers on a 24-hour basis is necessary in the event that the corporate aircraft uses a remote airfield with limited operations and minimal security or is parked in a remote area of a major airport.

Local Transportation

- The use of public transportation such as taxis, buses, and subways is not recommended.

- A four-door sedan should be available for use throughout the visit. Care should be taken to ensure that the vehicle is unobtrusive, so as not to bring undue attention to the visitor. The chauffeur or driver, if used, should be bilingual and knowledgeable of the local area and routes to be traveled.

Accommodations

- Hotel reservations should be booked at a first-class hotel located in a low-crime area. Hotel management need not be contacted to provide unusual security or other arrangements for the visitor. A low-key approach is essential to ensure anonymity. Reference to the company or the visitor's position should be avoided.

- Visitors should be preregistered to avoid being required to check in at the reception desk. The room key should be provided to the visitor immediately upon his or her arrival at the hotel or airport by personnel responsible for coordinating the visit.

- The guest room or suite should be located between the second and seventh floor of the hotel, preferably on a floor with a separate concierge. The room should be away from the public elevator lobby but near an emergency exit.

- Valuables should be stored in accordance with hotel safekeeping provisions.

- Use of a guesthouse or private residence is acceptable as long as it is not located in an isolated area.

Official Functions and Activities

- Coordinate all activities and visit sites before the visitor's attendance. The coordinator should obtain guest lists and detailed itineraries, determine emergency evacuation routes, and ascertain the purpose of the function.

- The coordinator should ensure that the function or activity does not subject the visitor to undue risk.

- Official company functions should be on an invitational basis and guests should be required to present their invitations at a reception desk staffed by company personnel before being granted access to the function. The receptionist should match the invitation to the guest list.

Liaison With Local Authorities

Prior to a visit by a VIP, you should make contact with the appropriate local authorities to advise them of the upcoming visit and to ascertain whether the current local security environment necessitates an upgraded security posture for the visit.

Background Data

An information packet should be prepared before the visit and presented to the executive upon his/her arrival. Information provided should include:

- Emergency telephone contact list, including company personnel (home and office numbers), hospital, police, fire, emergency services, and company doctor;

- Maps of the area;

- Detailed itinerary;

- Availability of company transportation;

- Brief review of current security situation including curfews, government-imposed restrictions, description of high-crime areas to be avoided, and other relevant factors; and

- Explanation of local currency (exchange rates and currency control laws or regulations).

Other

- Details of visits by VIPs should be considered company confidential and distribution limited on a need-to-know basis.

- Media coverage, unless requested by the visitor, is unwarranted.

Moderate Threat-Factors and Guidelines

Moderate Threat Factors

Factors which should be used by management in determining whether in view of the local security environment a moderate threat potential exists include the following:

- Stable local government;

- Effective law enforcement;

- Some history of terrorist attacks against multinational companies and/or their executives;

- No previous history of criminal or terrorist acts directed against company executives;

- Upswing in criminal activity, particularly violent crimes with some history of criminal kidnappings for financial gain;

- Some current adverse publicity against the company and potential for nonviolent groups to protest against company policies during the executive's visit.

Moderate Threat Guidelines

Unarmed Security Escort

In addition to the guidance set forth in "Minimal Threat Guidelines," an unarmed security escort should be used when a determination is made by management that a moderate threat exists.

High Threat-Factors and Guidelines

High Threat Factors

Factors which should be used by management in determining whether in view of the local security environment a high threat potential exists include the following:

- Unstable or unpopular local government, with terrorist groups actively attempting to bring about its overthrow;

- Ineffective or corrupt law enforcement agencies unable to reduce criminal activity and bring the terrorist problem under control;

- Significant history of terrorist attacks against multinational companies and/or their executives, including bombings, assassinations, and kidnappings;

- Recent history of criminal or terrorist acts or threats against company facilities and/or their executives;

- Widespread criminal activity reaching all elements of local society with emphasis on violent crimes;

- Considerable adverse publicity against company policies and organized local groups that have been leaning toward violence and are planning to protest company policies during the executive's visit;

- Other factors appropriate to the local environment. Asking the consulate regional security officer at the embassy is a good idea.

High Threat Guidelines

Recommendation Against Visit

High-threat potential means a significant risk to the well-being of the executive. You should strongly recommend against a visit by the executive if a high risk exists. By definition, this category will apply to a limited number of locations, but might vary based on the local situation at a particular point in time. For example, a potential visit might be deemed a moderate risk one month and high risk another because of changes in the local environment.

Armed Protective Security Detail

If the executive cannot be dissuaded from visiting the high threat area, an armed protective security detail should be used.

Specific guidelines for high-risk protective details are beyond the scope of this document because of the multiple and various considerations in organizing each individual protective detail. However, the use of trained security professionals is essential.

The items covered in "Minimal Threat Guidelines", will still have to be addressed when an armed protective detail is required. However, the manner in which relevant tasks are performed may be modified by guidelines issued in regard to the armed details. Some general guidelines are as follows:

- Professional bodyguards dressed in plainclothes and equipped with weapons and two-way radios should accompany the executive at all times. At least one bodyguard should remain in the direct vicinity of the executive whenever potential public contact is envisioned.

- Security personnel should conduct advance surveys of all sites to be visited and be on the scene throughout the executive's visit to the location.

- Security personnel should be assigned to the hotel or residence on a 24-hour basis to ensure that unauthorized individuals do not enter the room or suite. Cleaning staff should be escorted whenever they enter the accommodations. The room or suite should be periodically checked to ensure that contraband (such as a bomb) has not been introduced into the area.

- An escort car or cars should be used on all vehicular movements by the executive to provide a response capacity in the event of an attack or vehicular mishap or breakdown. The escort car or cars should be staffed by at least two security professionals.

- The executive's vehicle should be driven by a security professional trained in evasive or defensive maneuvers. The vehicle should be inspected before use to ensure that explosive devices have not been installed on the vehicle or that the vehicle has not been otherwise tampered with by unauthorized individuals. Use of an armored car, if available, is recommended.

- Public exposure should be limited to the minimum necessary for the executive to complete his or her assignment.

Group Activities Guidelines

The exposure created by a number of executives gathering at a single location necessitates some degree of increased security. The following is a list of some general guidelines for use in such group activities:

- The suites should be inspected before occupancy to ensure that no contraband or unauthorized individuals are located in the rooms.

- Security should be provided for corporate aircraft overnighting at the local airport. Such security may be provided by off-duty uniformed and armed police officers or contract security guards.

- The hotel activity boards should make no reference to the company. Publicity and press coverage should be minimized. A low profile is strongly recommended. Anonymity is a powerful ally of a traveling executive.

- If possible, hotel guest rooms occupied by company personnel should be located in one section of the hotel. Consideration should be given to hiring a security officer to patrol the hallway in the vicinity of the guest rooms and function rooms during hours of darkness or even on a 24-hour basis.

- Access to functions should be controlled to prevent an unauthorized individual from gaining access to the meetings or functions. This can be handled by assigning a member of the meeting staff to serve as a receptionist outside the door. Access can be granted either by personal recognition or by checking identity cards.

- Information packets provided to participants should include the name and telephone number of the staff person responsible for security. Staff personnel should be provided with an emergency contact list, including the telephone numbers of the nearest hospital with an emergency room, ambulance service, police department, and fire department.

- Consideration should be given to leasing pagers to ensure that staff personnel can be rapidly contacted in the event of an emergency.

- Upon the conclusion of the meeting, staff personnel should inspect all guest rooms and function rooms to ensure that no documents, personal effects, or equipment have been left behind by participants.

Appendix I. Security Survey Checklist

General, Preparatory Data

1.   Site name, address, telephone number:

Please fill in the name of the people holding the following positions:

Manager

Assistant Manager

Human Resources Manager

Person responsible for site security

Number of Employees

Area Covered/Office Size

Operating Hours

Function

2.   Survey should include review of theft reports prepared by this site for an appropriate prior period. Where appropriate, has corrective action been

taken?
Do theft reports reflect patterns, trends, or particular problems at this location?

3. What does site management regard as the most prevalent or serious security problem?

4. Does the site maintain items of value, such as works of art, paintings, wall hangings, etc.?

5. What are the site's most valuable physical assets?

6. Does the location have an employees' handbook or manual or other means of enumerating rules of conduct?
Have employees been notified that violation of these rules are grounds for disciplinary action up to and including discharge?
Do these rules of conduct include theft of company, customer, and employee property, including information?

7. Identify off-site locations that should be included in survey, to include warehouses, offices, storage facilities, etc.
Are these locations protected against vandalism and theft?

8. What is the police agency having jurisdiction over the site?
   Does the plant have a dedicated telephone line to this agency?
   Have they been called for assistance in the recent past?
   What has been their response?
   Do they normally include any of our perimeter in their patrols?
   If requested, would they?

9. Are police emergency numbers readily available to personnel who should have this information?

10. Is information readily available on how to reach the proper agency for assistance with illegal narcotics, bomb threats, obscene calls, etc.?
    Do you have a policy of reporting identifiable items of stolen property to the local police for addition to their files, indexes?

11. Some police agencies have a Crime Prevention Unit that responds to invitations to speak on various topics (drugs, rape, etc.) or that may conduct limited security surveys.
    Is this service available?
    If so, have you taken advantage of it?

Perimeter Security

Lighting Evaluation

12. Is the perimeter adequately lighted?

13. Does lighting aid or inhibit guards in the performance of their duties?

14. Is lighting compatible with closed-circuit television (CCTV)?
    Does it cause monitor to "bloom"?

15. Is the power supply adequately protected?

16. Is lighting properly maintained and cleaned?

17. Are sensitive areas (parking lots, computer areas, stores, storage rooms, shipping/receiving areas) adequately lighted?

18. If an emergency occurred, is the site adequately lighted?
    Is the fenceline adequately lighted?
    In appropriate areas, is glare projection lighting used?

Security Force

19. Proprietary?
    Contract?

If contract, name of agency and telephone number If proprietary, what is method and source of selection of personnel?

20. Are perimeter patrols conducted? Frequency?

21. Is an incident log, including alarms/responses maintained? Reviewed daily?
By Whom?

22. Are security personnel used for non-security related duties?
If yes, what duties?

23. Does site use photo ID cards? Compatible with access control system? Who administers it?

24. Are all employees required to show photo ID card upon entry? Is duplicate copy kept on file?

25. Are parking decals or other methods of registering employee vehicles used? Are privately owned vehicles permitted to park on site? If so, can an individual reach a vehicle without passing a guard?

26. Does the site have a receptionist in place at all times? Are visitors required to register?

Are they provided with an identifying badge, and are non-company employees escorted while on the site? Is visitor identification verified (e.g., vending company ID, etc.)?

Perimeter Protection

27. If outside building walls form part of the perimeter, are all doors and windows secured against surreptitious entry? Can entry be achieved via the roof? Can hinge pins be removed from doors? Are all entry/egress points controlled when opened?

Internal Security

Lock/Key Control

28. With whom does physical and administrative key control rest?

29. Is a master key system in use?
How many grandmaster/master keys have been issued?
Is adequate control exercised over these keys?

30. Is a cross-control system (name versus key number) in use?
What type of numbering system is in use?

Is the entire system, including blanks, inventoried on a regular basis?
Are they stamped "Do Not Duplicate"?

31. What level of management authorization (written?) is required for issuance of keys?

32. Identify personnel who are permitted to have keys to perimeter fence, doors.

33. Are office/facility keys, particularly masters, permitted to be taken home?
Are keys signed in/out in a daily log?

34. Are locks rotated?

35. How long has the present lock/key system been in use?
Have keys been reported lost?
What level key?
What is the policy when this happens?

36. Is a record of locations of safes and their combinations maintained?
Are combinations routinely changed annually and when an individual who knows one no longer has that need to know? (separation, transfer, retirement)
Are safe combinations, if written, maintained in a secure place?

Alarms and Electronics

37. What type, if any, electronic security system is in use here?
    Do alarms terminate at the site or at an outside central station?
    Has service/response been satisfactory?

38. List alarms such as burglar (doors, windows, space (motion)), duress (receptionist, cashier, nurse), other (card access, CCTV, etc.)

Theft Control Procedures

39. Does the site have a policy of marking items susceptible to theft (calculators, office equipment, hand tools, microwave ovens, TV monitors, VCRs, etc.) so they can be identified as company property?
    Describe the extent of the program.
    Does it include die stamping or etching and painting?

40. Are serial numbers of all items bearing them recorded?
    In the event of theft, is this information related to the police for inclusion in stolen property indexes, and for identification and return in case of subsequent recovery?

41. Are trash receptacles periodically inspected to determine whether items of value may be removed from the site via them?

42. Are all store/office supplies, etc., attended when open?
    What is the procedure for drawing supplies when no attendant is present?

43. Are telephone records properly safeguarded to prevent unauthorized destruction?
    Is access to telephone switching equipment (the "frame room") restricted?

44. Who performs custodial services - proprietary or contract janitorial people?
    Is access limited to the office area only?
    Are they bonded?
    Are they required to wear ID badges?
    Are they checked during the performance of their duties?
    Are they inspected by guards as they leave?
    Are the janitors' vehicles inspected on the way off the property?
    How is trash removed from the site?
    Are the vehicles used to remove trash inspected on the way off the property?
    Do the janitors have access to restricted or sensitive areas?
    Are they given office keys (masters?)?

Are they permitted to take these keys off the site with them?

45. How much cash is kept on site? Is it handled at more than one location?
How is cash supply replenished?
Where is it kept during working hours?
Where is it kept after hours?
Where are blank payroll checks kept?
Where are blank disbursement checks kept?
Considering the neighborhood the site is located in, and the amount of cash on site, how do you assess your vulnerability to armed robbery or burglary?

Proprietary/Limited Information

46. Is there Proprietary and/or Limited data on site?
If so, in what form?
Is it properly marked?
Is it stored in a secure location?
Are the following locked at the end of the day:

a. Offices?

b. Filing Cabinets?

c. Desks?

47. What are office destruction procedures and file purging for Proprietary data?

48. Does the site have a clean desk policy?

Personnel Security

49. Are any background checks conducted prior to employment? Are previous employment dates verified? Are personnel medical records properly safeguarded? Is security included in the new hire orientation? Is company property (credit cards, ID keys) retrieved during exit interviews?

Emergency Procedures

50. Do you have a current bomb threat procedure?
Who implements it? (searches areas)
Does the procedure include a checklist for the switchboard operator?

51. Is there a contingency plan for acts of violence?
A disaster plan?

52. If personnel are required to work alone, are they periodically checked by someone to ascertain their well-being?

What means do they have of calling for help in an emergency?

Computer Security

53. Are terminated employees immediately separated from the EDP function?

54. Is access to the data center controlled physically, electronically?
Locked when not in use?

55. Is output distributed via user-controlled lock boxes? Is tape library maintained physically separate from machine room?

Threat Information

56. Has liaison been established by your office with the American Embassy Regional Security Officer (RSO)?
Is the RSO able to notify you of security threats concerning known terrorist groups active in the area?
Any groups that harbor hatred for U.S. corporations, your company, its manager, and employees?
Anniversary dates that local population or terrorist groups celebrate?
What tactics and activities are practiced or adopted by local terrorist groups that might

affect your company, its managers and employees?

57. Do you have sources that will inform you of any political controversy or labor disputes that might impact your operations?

58. Will you provide Security with copies of information, that may be detrimental to the company, received as a result of your contacts with the RSO, as well as other sources, including newspaper articles?

Appendix II. Facility Questionnaire

1. Are there any known groups that harbor hatred for U.S. businesses, managers and employees?
   Identify:

2. What terrorist groups are known to be active in the area?
   What tactics have these groups been known to use?
   What is the possibility of a change in these tactics?

3. Are there known groups that vocally oppose foreign capitalism or imperialism in

the area?
Identify:

4. Are there any known groups that vocally or actively oppose the local government that the United States supports?
Identify:

5. Is there any current political controversy or labor dispute that we should be aware of?

6. Are there any upcoming anniversary dates that the local population or terrorist groups celebrate? Identify:

7. Have there been any previous hostage taking or kidnapping incidents, bombings, assassinations, strikes against U.S. businesses or the government, demonstrations, assaults, sabotage against corporate facilities or products, or occupation of corporate facilities in the area?
Identify:

8. If there have been previous hostage taking or kidnapping incidents,

   a. How were the victims seized?

   b. What was the fate of the hostages?

   c. How much ransom was demanded?

d. Was it paid?

e. How were the negotiations handled?

9. Does the host country prohibit negotiating with hostage takers or prohibit the payment of ransom?

10. Do you consider the local police and intelligence services effective?

11. What are the aims of the local criminals or terrorist groups?
What tactics or type of activity by these groups would best further those aims?

12. What is the identified groups' capability of carrying out planned activities such as ambush, hostage taking, kidnapping, execution, bombing, etc.?

13. In the event of terrorist activity, which organizations, businesses, groups, or individuals would be the most likely targets?

Appendix III. Threatening Phone Call Checklist

PLACE THIS UNDER YOUR TELEPHONE - BOMB THREAT!

QUESTIONS TO ASK:

1. When is bomb going to explode?

2. Where is it right now?

3. What does it look like?

4. What kind of bomb is it?

5. What will cause it to explode?

6. Did you place the bomb?

7. Why?

8. What is your address?

9. What is your name?

EXACT WORDING OF THE THREAT:

Sex of caller:

Race:

Age:

Length of Call:

Number at which call is received:

Time: Date: /   /

CALLER'S VOICE:

Calm	Nasal
Angry	Stutter
Excited	Lisp
Slow	Raspy
Rapid	Deep
Soft	Ragged
Loud	Clearing throat
Laughter	Deep breathing
Crying	Cracking voice
Normal	Disguised
District	Accent
Slurred	Familiar

If voice is familiar, who did it sound like?

BACKGROUND SOUNDS:

Voices	Street noises
Crockery	Animal noises
Clear	PA System
Static	Music

    Local   House noises

    Booth   Long distance

    Motor   Other

    Factory machinery

    Office machinery

THREAT LANGUAGE:

    Well spoken   Incoherent

    (educated)   Taped

    Foul   Irrational

    Message read by threat maker

REMARKS:

Report call immediately to:

Phone number

Date / /

Name

Position

Phone number

HOSTAGE!

QUESTIONS TO ASK:

2. Who is this?

3. Where are you calling from?

4. Is this a prank?

5. How do I know this is not a prank?

6. May I talk to the hostage?

7. Is the hostage all right?

8. What do you want?

VERY IMPORTANT:

9. Will you call back in 15 minutes?

10. How can I contact you if I have trouble meeting your demands?

EXACT WORDING OF DEMAND:

Sex of Caller: Race:

Age: Length of call:

Number at which call is received:

Time: Date: /   /

Appendix IV. Letter and Parcel Bomb Recognition Points

WARNING!

LETTER AND PARCEL BOMB RECOGNITION POINTS

- Foreign Mail, Air Mail, and Special Delivery
- Restrictive Markings, such as Confidential, Personal, Etc.
- Excessive Postage
- Hand Written or Poorly Typed Addresses
- Incorrect Titles
- Titles but No Names
- Misspellings of Common Words
- Oily Stains or Discolorations
- No Return Address
- Excessive Weight
- Rigid Envelope
- Lopsided or Uneven Envelope
- Protruding Wires or Tinfoil

- Excessive Securing Material, such as Masking Tape, String, etc.
- Visual Distractions

Made in the USA
Middletown, DE
29 June 2022